TABLE OF CONTEN

MW01147378

Dedication:

To all the courageous dreamers that have taken responsibility for their futures by starting their own business. Becoming a successful entrepreneur is the solution to America's challenges. This book was written to honor you!

Forward / Special Note

Have you ever wondered how ordinary people accomplish extraordinary things? This book is a personal accounting of the journey that several of the greatest business leaders of our era went through to make that transformation. These incredible people answer a series of the most often asked questions in a candid story that could enlighten, educate and empower any reader. Each chapter is focused on one person's journey to become a person of influence. As the answers to pointed questions unfold, you will learn how to overcome adversity and handle the challenges that everyone must face to become a leader.

All of the leaders within the pages of this book came from very different backgrounds. By most standards observed by society today, they should not be successful or at the helm of organizations numbering in the thousands, but they are. What exactly did they do? Who were their inspirations? What kept them going during the tough times? If they were to start all over today, what would they do differently? What advice would they give to a brand new entrepreneur? What advice would they give to a veteran in business? What is their vision of the future? These questions and many more will be answered in this unique book, specifically designed for ambitious people with a burning desire to become a leader.

Before reading this book, stop and ask yourself which challenges have you been struggling with lately. What might be holding YOU back? Why aren't people responding to you the way that you want them to? Prepare your mind to receive the answers through relating to the situations and stories of these great people. I believe we were all made to be great and were given the ability to accomplish whatever our heart desires. Somewhere along the way, we were convinced otherwise and stopped believing and dreaming. Everything great in life begins with a dream!

Dan & Pat,

It's great to be your business partner & friend.

You're a Power Couple!

See You at the Top!

Chapter 1
Jeff Levitan

I grew up in Chicago in a lower-middle-income family. My father was a truck driver, my mom was a waitress, and we, like most families in America, struggled financially. I watched my parents fight about money most of my life and a lot of my memories of childhood revolved around the stress and struggles that we went through as a family. By the time I was 17, my parents had divorced and I was left wondering what my future had in store for me.

Growing up experiencing the lack of financial security, I knew my future had to be different. Tony Robbins talks about people being motivated only by one of two things: the desire for gain or pleasure, or the avoidance of pain. I was totally motivated by the avoidance of pain. Without knowing how, I knew why I needed to make a lot of money and end up financially secure. I was set on having enough money so that I wouldn't argue with, fight with, or deny my family a loving, peaceful life.

Although most people in my neighborhood were stuck there, I knew that I wanted to make something great of my life. Unfortunately, I was told, like many people, if you get a good education and you are well-rounded, that you might be able to get a good job at a decent company someday. What an outdated idea that is today.

I tried to get good grades and I played sports hoping to garner a scholarship. Unfortunately, by the time I was ready to go to college, a scholarship was not offered to me and my parents couldn't afford to send me to any good colleges. I ended up at community college my first year and then later transferred to Illinois State University, a big state school that was inexpensive, made more affordable with student loans and government grants. I was the typical student, studied a little and partied a lot. I also boxed for a few years in college to alleviate my worldly frustrations.

When I finished college, I did what a lot of people do: I put thousands of resumes out there, hoping for a company to pick me and choose me for a job. After many interviews and no call-backs, I finally had one company decide that they would accept me into their training program. They moved me up to Minnesota, which was a colder, smaller, and less exciting location than Chicago. Upon entering the program, I was told I could choose any three territories around the country to work from after completing the program. I picked California, Texas or Florida.

When I finished the program one year later, they sent me to Milwaukee, Wisconsin. I had asked myself, "God, why did I end up here? How did I end up here?" To me, Milwaukee was a little suburb north of Chicago. After about a year of being in a place I didn't want to be, doing a job I really didn't want to do, I got my answer. I was watching people in my company that were there five to ten years longer than me; they were flat out miserable. I knew I needed to get out while I was still young and positive.

One fateful day a friend of mine that lived in my apartment complex told me about this great business that he was involved in. It was an opportunity to be my own boss and determine my own income. He brought me to his office and it was unlike anything I had seen before. All of the walls were coated with plaques and trophies like a sports hall of fame museum. The office was also full of happy people, smiling and greeting each other like a family reunion. I suddenly became the center of attention and everyone wanted to meet me. It was very unusual, but it did feel good.

Everyone kept talking about this guy Greg Kapp that I needed to meet. When I finally met him, he was so well edified that I was a little nervous. Luckily, he was very kind and down to earth. He ultimately was the person to interview me. At no time did I ever get the impression that this was a join type of business. Greg asked me a lot of tough questions, making me qualify myself for the position. At one point, he even told me that I was probably too young and not at a stage in my life to be serious about business; that only made me want it more.

I remember Mr. Kapp asking me how much I thought I was worth per year. I thought it was a trick question and, at the time, I was earning about 40k per year in my job. I told him I thought I was worth around 75k per year. He snapped back, "I'm not even going to work with you if you think that little of yourself!" I was taken aback. I responded, "Well, I meant to say 100k." He shook his head and said, "I'm going to start you on probation until you prove yourself. You better do exactly what I ask of you or I'm passing you off to someone else." I responded, "Yes, Sir." You see, I think how you start someone and set expectations for them is everything. At that time, I was looking for a new career and Greg sensed that. You can't say the wrong thing to the right person. I was that right person because I was looking for something new. It didn't matter what they said to me or how they said it, I was interested.

When I got into this business, I was told right off the bat that I was too young, I was only 24 years old, and I probably wasn't going to make it. Friends and family did not support me either right away. They told me to keep my real job. They said it wasn't going to work; some even said the company wasn't real or legitimate. I chose not to listen to the negativity and decided that I was going to prove them all wrong. I worked diligently every evening and weekend and was driven to make this work. What I realized later was that most people are afraid to try something new or think outside of the box. They are like crabs in a bucket. Every time one ambitiously tries to climb out, the others pull them back in!

One thing that was so attractive to me was that I didn't have to quit my job to give this business a try. Most companies in the financial field make you quit your job; it's all or nothing, sink or swim, and most people sink. Having the opportunity to do this part-time allowed me to bridge that uncomfortable gap at the beginning; it let me get comfortable with the business, to get comfortable with myself, to get comfortable with selling and comfortable with a new industry.

It only took a few months and I started making a decent part-time income. The extra $1,000-$2,000 per month made all the difference in the world at that point of my life. It was only a few months after that and I was making more money part-time than my full-time job. What a great experience that was. I was able to go to my boss and basically tell him that he was fired. That was one of the greatest times of my life; to be able to take control of my own future, to be my own boss, and to actually have a little taste of the American dream, which is owning your own business.

During my first six months, I was commuting back and forth three to four times per week all the way from Milwaukee to Chicago, which was a two hour drive in each direction. You would think it was a nightmare but I turned it into an opportunity. I got involved in, and kind of obsessed with these things called self-development books-on-tape. I began listening to books every trip, both ways. It took about two hours to listen to a book. So, on my way to Chicago, I'd listen to a book, and on my way home I would listen to another book.

I learned more in those six months than I had learned in my prior 24 years. It was a different type of learning too. It was wisdom, not knowledge. There were things on those tapes that all the books in school never taught. I was a sponge, ready to be a new man. I was ready to grow and change, and I was primed to do great things in life and in this business. I realized that the difference between most people in this world was not their looks, social status, interests, or vocation; it's the roughly six inch space between their ears. The way we think determines everything we are and will ever be.

One of the most useful things on tape I listened to was the BPM presentation given by Rich Thawley in the early 90's. I wore it out on my many trips to Chicago, practicing explaining our opportunity in a simple yet powerful way. It still serves me to this day. Another thing I greatly appreciated was the fact that there was a simple, proven system to follow. Greg Kapp gave me the book and told me to treat it like it's gold. He said it was derived by trial and error over the past 20 years. Greg told me this business was more about duplicating and less about creating.

I followed what was in that book and sure enough, my first year full-time, which was 1996, I made well over $100,000 in income. I earned the coveted $100k ring. I proved all my family and friends wrong. As a matter of fact, I was so fired up that I made a copy of my 1099 tax form showing my income that year and mailed it and faxed it to all my naysayers and doubters. Another one of the best days of my life was proving everybody wrong. The best days of my life seemed to keep happening over and over.

My first year after making $100,000, I bought my mom a new car, I took my dad to Hawaii, and then for the next five years I took my grandfather to Hawaii. Being blessed and fortunate enough to have one grandparent left alive, I got to spend many days and weeks with him, and he became one of my best friends and mentors. He is a World War II veteran, a Chicago firefighter, and went to all my football games when I was a kid. He was my hero in many different ways and it was an honor to show him how important he was to me. Taking him to Hawaii all those times was just a great way to express it. We all have someone in our lives that we appreciate so much that we would love to do something amazing for. Tomorrow is not promised to any of us and we ought to hurry up and do what our heart is telling us to!

Like most people that grew up broke, I wanted to feel what being rich was like. I started buying houses, fancy cars, Rolex watches, and other displays of success and wealth. Eventually, what I realized was that there was a law of diminishing returns with those things. The more money I made didn't necessarily have the power to keep making me more fulfilled. It was just another house that I spent little time in or another car that I rarely drove or another watch that sat in my drawer. What was the point? Ultimately, it was fun to experience but it didn't fulfil me. I finally realized what really fulfilled me was making a difference in the lives of other people.

At the age of 30, while I was in a period of semi-retirement, I came up with the idea of giving back by starting a children's charity called All For One. I was going to help the most underprivileged people in the world, which are orphans in third world countries. I started this charity much like I started this business: with many naysayers and Doubting Thomas' who told me it wouldn't work.

So, I did exactly what I did to start this business. I created a system of doing presentations and recruiting people who had experience and talent that I did not have. I found people that had worked for the American Red Cross before and we put together a mission trip to Nicaragua. We went down there and partnered with Save The Children and Care International, two well-respected and established charities. We did a lot of great things for underprivileged children in that country.

Then we took video footage from the mission, brought it back, and showed the entire organization and team. They were so moved that many of my business partners and leaders joined the board of directors, and we were off to do things in Haiti, the Philippines, and Vietnam. We built a child prosperity center, essentially an orphanage, in Uganda for over 100 children and now have the adjoining school under way. Founding All For One and making such a profound impact on the lives of so many children is one of the things I am most proud of in my life.

Meeting My Spouse In The Business

A few years later, in early 2007, I met my wife and my life partner, Cam, at a company convention. She was in the business, working out of an office in California. One good thing about this business is that there are lots of people that have similar interests, goals, and values. So, when you meet somebody in this organization, you have a great opportunity to meet somebody equally yoked. If you're already committed, make sure your partner is involved. If you're single, you have a great chance to find your dream partner here. Side note: The more successful you are, the greater the selection becomes! Cam and I found each other and started our family in 2008. Today, we have four beautiful children and counting. They are getting the chance to live the life that I always wished I could've grown up living. Most importantly, they are being raised in an environment full of people I admire and trust!

What Are The Keys To My Personal Success?

There are many keys to personal success. I think success has a recipe; it doesn't matter if it's this business or any other business. Success leaves clues, and some of those clues are discipline, accountability, specific goals, and drive. Those are the attributes that really move people and make you commit to things that, normally, you wouldn't commit to. I also believe that knowing which direction you're going in is important from the start. Many people start and stop and start over again. Every time you restart, it requires so much energy to get momentum going again. One of the keys to success is making a well thought out decision one time and going all the way to your destination, not stopping until you get there. Measure twice, cut once.

My Advice To A New Associate

If I were to give advice to someone that was brand new, I would tell them to be cautious from whom they get their advice. First, only listen to the people that are supportive of their goals and dreams. The people we really need giving us advice are people who care about us and our future. Everybody out there has an opinion and opinions are usually worth what we pay for them, nothing. We need to avoid small-thinking pessimists. They never accomplish much and usually lead dissatisfying lives of mediocrity. Also, make sure that you take advice from people that are where you want to be in life, accomplished and happy. If they're not where you want to be in life, why would you take advice from them, except maybe to serve as a warning of what not to do?

Another piece of advice I would give to somebody new is to follow the system. Millions of people have come through this organization and had many degrees of success and failure. They have tried most everything you could imagine. Some things work well while others work infrequently and to a small measure. So, by trial and error, our system manual was invented. Our Business Format System literally is a publication of what has been proven to work the most often and with the highest degree of success. The danger is that everything can work to a degree, but the things that work best are in that manual; so follow that manual. Otherwise, you will waste an enormous amount of time and energy doing things that keep you busy, but don't produce substantial results.

New people need to be coachable. By design, our compensation system in our company attaches and aligns your leader's compensation to yours. So, if you make a lot of money, your leader makes a percentage of a lot of money; if you make zero, they make a percentage of zero. They have a vested interest in you becoming very, very successful. So, be coachable and understand that, while no one is perfect, your leader's intentions are to see you become successful.

Last piece of advice for new people; make sure you attend all the big events. It is well understood that this business is built from big event to big event. The main reason is that most people struggle with their belief in this business or, more importantly, belief in themselves. Conventions and big events help increase people's belief and understanding. It's hard to convince someone if you're not convinced. The most frequent excuse I get for not attending is the financial obligation. Many times it's only $50-$150 for a three-day event but for some, it's a stretch. They say, "I can't afford to go." I say, "You can't afford not to." If you are a full-grown adult and don't have a few hundred dollars to your name, something is severely wrong. Something has to change. A major shift in thinking must occur and that usually happens at our big events.

My Advice To A Leader Who Is Stuck In A Rut

If you are a leader and you have been around for a long time and you are stuck, what you need to do immediately is set some new goals and recommit all over again. Act like a brand new person one more time. It's usually that crucial enthusiasm that is missing. I know that you probably have the licenses and that you've got a lot of experience; you may even have somewhat of a team put together. None of those things really matter if you're not excited anymore. You need to let yourself be re-sold the dream like you are new. People do more when they are fired up. So, you've got to act like a fired up new person that just happens to have a lot of experience. Reset some goals that really motivate you to get out of bed in the morning. Forgive yourself for everything you did wrong or didn't do the first time and start all over again!

Common Mistakes Associates Make

There are several common mistakes that many people make in this business. One of them is listening to negative influences or people that steal dreams. Your associations determine your life. I wish I could sugarcoat it, but I can't. They say you become the average of the five people you spend the most time with. Choose wisely and associate with people that make you feel a little uncomfortable or challenged. I have never learned a thing from someone that has agreed with me! Make sure you spend your precious time with people that are ambitious and growth-oriented. This may mean disassociating, or at least reducing your time spent with certain friends or family members.

Another common mistake is spending time and energy trying to recreate the system. People spend millions of dollars in the franchise business every year to buy a proven system they can duplicate. Our proven system comes included with your inexpensive AMA fee. The key is to treat our system like you paid a million dollars for it. I was always told that we get paid here for duplication, not creation. Eric Olson says it's ok to be a copycat as long as you copy the right cat!

I think people sometimes don't practice what they preach. They tell everybody to get their finances in order, do a budget, and save money, but they don't do it themselves. Take your own medicine. I think we need to be careful not to become hypocritical or judgmental of anybody. Make sure that we do what we ask of others so that our own lives can serve as an example to others.

Not personally developing is another common mistake. I know one of the greatest keys to success was that drive I took three to four times per week and all the books I put into my brain along the way. I have found that for a lot of people whose businesses aren't growing, it's because they aren't growing. They stopped personally developing somewhere along the way. What our lives look like today is a direct reflection of who we are. If we want the things around us to change, we must start with changing the way we think. The way we think is who we are! One great suggestion is to continue making a personal development goal for yourself every year. If others don't notice that you're different, if no one comments on your change, you're probably the same old you!

My Personal Challenges

One of the most difficult challenges that I have ever had as a leader is when I try to change people. We are all where we are supposed to be in our lives at any given time. When you try to change people, they'll usually end up resenting you later, even if they change. Many times though, they won't change and it will wear you out. Love them for who they are. When they are ready to change, they will. You are better off bringing in brand new people that are very coachable, that desire to change and focus on them. Draw attention to the changes happening in the successful people and maybe that will influence them. Greg Kapp says, "Nothing can ever be taught; it always has to be caught." So, if you find yourself frustrated with your current people, get some new ones!

Things I would do Differently If I Had to Start Over

If I were to start all over again, one of the things I would do differently is to focus on the big picture from the beginning. The big picture is the race for outlets. An outlet, in our business, is a leader who can run their own operation. At first, I thought I was going to be a financial planner. Soon after, I became confused. "Should I be trying to go write business or trying to recruit people?" I would tell you, there's always more business to write, but there is a finite number of great leaders. There is a race for locations, a race for offices, and we should all be trying to find the leaders who can get that done. We should be talent scouts from day one. Some of the best people in this company were actually found, not built.

The leaders in this book all had a champion spirit within them when they got here. This company and its existing leaders may have cut and shaped them, but they were in fact already rough diamonds when they were found. How do you find diamonds and gold and other things precious? You have to mine thousands of tons of rock to get there. What I would tell you is that you have to be prepared and excited about the process, not just the results. The way that you are going to find champions and leaders is by bringing in lots of people and filtering the leaders from the masses. There is no way around it. Every leader has the potential of thousands of sales, but every sale does not have the potential of thousands of recruits. Be careful where you focus your efforts.

The Future

At this stage, we have laid the foundation for a game-changing company. We have the systems and leaders in place to accomplish the unlikely, if not the impossible. Financial freedom simply gives you numerous options and choices. You can often tell the character of a person by what they do when they don't need the money anymore. I would just tell you I am most proud of all my business partners, everybody that has been highlighted in this book. They are becoming great men and women of influence for their families and for their communities. Although many of the CEO's in this book are financially secure, they continue to show up, day-in and day-out, and lead by example. Most of these leaders have also banded together to do great things with the All For One Foundation as well as many other charities that are near and dear to their hearts, making big money and making a big impact for those less fortunate. What tremendous philanthropists!

We've all become great examples to those in our family and those under our influence. I'm excited about the way we can actually change an industry. I believe that our organization will continue to grow and impact our entire society for generations to come. The fact that we have the opportunity to be part of this during our one short lifetime is nothing short of exhilarating. If you take a look at the entire history of America and consider being part of a positive movement, maybe THE movement that can literally change the trajectory of the financial system in America, it's unbelievable. It is truly a blessing to be part of that crusade. To be on a championship team is great. To be a leader on a championship team is extraordinary. I am so proud to be associated with all the people in this book as well as those that have yet to be showcased in future volumes of *The Leadership Journey*.

Chapter 2

John Shin

Our family came here in the 1960s from South Korea seeking a different life and better opportunities. Though that was not an easy task, they made it to California. Of all the wonderful places in California we could have gone, we ended up in East L.A. and I grew up in an area called Rampart.

There were, for the most part, no Asians where I grew up. Then we moved to the city of Glendale where my sister and I were the only two Asian kids in the entire school. Obviously, we had a speaking and communication challenge. We couldn't understand them and they couldn't understand us. People looked at us differently because they had never seen Asian people before. It was as if it was the first time they had ever seen somebody of raw color, somebody who had slanted eyes. They were so intrigued by us that we were made fun of, got picked on, and were bullied. The teachers were not excited about having us in their classroom because they couldn't communicate with us. They even brought our parents in and told them that they wanted to put us in learning disability classes with children who really did have disabilities. We had no friends and felt isolated. We didn't think that was the American dream. It was not why we left home, what we came to this country for.

Long story short, my parents put me in martial arts to make sure that I learned how to protect myself in the event that I was bullied again. Sending me to a martial arts school was probably the best decision my parents made. Our master would tell us every day that we were incredible people, that we were somebody, that we going to grow to become great leaders someday, that we were here learning martial arts, and that we were protectors and guardians.

Eventually, I became so good at martial arts that my master told us that that I should start competing. I had no idea how to compete. I'd never competed and we had been trained to protect and guard people. Suddenly, I was going into a tournament and now my objective was to hurt people, my competition, which was quite different from how we were trained. I struggled a little bit trying to figure out what I was supposed to do. I think that was huge because our master told us a lot of stuff about martial arts and the philosophy of being patient to acquire things. Most people never made it to black belt. Many tried for a year or two year before quitting; it took 6 1/2 years at our school to get a black belt. So, for 6 1/2 years, you are wondering if you're ever going to get there. You are a kid and you want this black belt because it's just the best thing to ever get; but, we learned to be patient.

We also learned about respect and to respect people all of the time, no matter what. The next thing he taught us was about listening; that we had to learn to listen more than we actually talked. The truth is: Most people want people to hear what they have to say but most people don't want to listen to what other people have to say. Even if you did want to talk, you had not proven yourself so why would people even want to listen to you? You didn't have anything that people wanted other than a black belt. The other students listened to you, but no one outside the school ever listened to you. Still, earning the black belt was a big thing for me; because of that, I really transformed my thinking and realized that I was somebody and that I was going to be a leader someday.

Then I went to college at USC — the University of Southern California — and I got my degree in Business Administration with an emphasis in marketing and a minor in political science. I got recruited by Coca-Cola. What I was getting paid was good, I initially thought, but then it wasn't as good as I thought it was because they took out so much in taxes. I went back to my counselor to visit with her and I told her that this corporate thing was not what I expected it to be. She said, "Maybe you should go get your MBA."

At that time, I decided that I didn't really want to go back to school again. My buddies and I felt that we were guardians and protectors — because that's what we were told; that we were here to protect people. I decided, along with a group of friends who all had black belts in martial arts, that we should become FBI and CIA agents. We would protect America; that we'd become secret agents and become assassins. So we applied to the FBI and CIA and our recruiters told us that to have a better opportunity to become a federal agent or CIA agent, we needed to have a postgraduate degree; specifically, a juris doctorate degree. I went back to my counselor and I said, "Do you know if I can get a JD at this school?" and she said, "Absolutely. In fact, there is an MBA JD program." I said, "Do you think that is something I can do?" She said, "I would not even put you in that program if I didn't think you could do it." So, I went into the JD MBA program, which is basically law school — that is typically three years — and the MBA, which is typically another two years. I got my JD MBA in just four years, though. Then I went and got a job in the District Attorney's Office in Orange County.

I met my wife, Arlene, in 1994. Arlene was in the mortgage and real estate business and one of her co-workers, Lynn, had a husband named Tom who flew from Chicago out to California to open up a financial services business and he recruited my wife into the business. Of course, I was a big skeptic. I didn't believe in the business; it was all sales and there were people and I didn't want to be around people.

Despite my skepticism, I joined the business in June of 1995, and that month, I went to the convention. That was it, I came back and I said, "This is where I want to be." I quit my job and I jumped into the business full-time, only to find out that I had to get some licenses. It took me nine months to get a license. Since I had quit my job and I didn't have any income, I actually ended up working at Claim Jumper restaurant in City of Industry, California. With a BS, a JD, and an MBA, I took a job as a waiter, making minimum wage plus tips, so that I could do this business. After work, I would go back to the office, change my clothes in the parking lot, wash up and shave in the bathroom at the office, put on a suit and tie, and then go greet people as they were coming to meetings and that's how I started this business.

When I joined this business, the office I was in was 98 % Korean and Asian people who didn't speak English very well and so they said, "John, since you're the best English speaker, you're doing the BPM." I said, "What is that?" They said, "You are doing the corporate overview," and I said, "What is that?" They said, "You are going to sell the dream," and I said, "What is that?" They said, "There is this presentation and you are going to do it." I said, "Okay."

As I did my very first BPM, I was sweating bullets. People started walking out because I was reading word for word off the PowerPoint slide. As people were leaving, it pissed me off and I thought: *I'm going to perfect this. I'm going to become an awesome speaker so that people stay. I'm going to do whatever I've got to do to entertain them so that they feel like they're getting some entertainment and some value.* So, I learned how to become funny in my presentations so people didn't quit, and the rest is history.

What Are The Keys To My Personal Success?

I think one of my keys to personal success is I am a ferocious competitor. I absolutely hate to lose and I've been like that since I was a kid. If I was on a team and I was playing baseball or basketball or kickball, even if I was playing chess with one of my buddies, or Monopoly or Candy Land with my own children during the holidays, I wanted to win. I wanted to be number one. I wanted to be the best and I think that that I was so obsessed with being number one; that I didn't want to lose was a major key.

I think I'm pretty structured. I think I'm one that needs to have some organization. I don't like chaos and that's why I don't like going to clubs; when I go to a club, it seems like it's out of control. I don't like going where there are a lot people because it just doesn't seem like there is any control there. So, I like to be in a controlled environment. I like to have organization. I need to be structured, so I'm very particular about my goals. Knowing that I have certain goals and that I have a purpose, is huge for me because I know that I'm going to hit those things, no matter what. I don't like to say that I'm going to do something and then not deliver it because I almost feel like I failed; not that I failed others, but that I failed myself because I didn't deliver what I said I was going to do.

My Advice To A New Associate

For a new person who is getting started in this business, I think what they should really do is trust their leader and know that the leader and his team is not there to waste their time but to help; the leader also benefits from the grooming that they do. It's in the leader's best interest to help the new person to succeed. So, the new person should trust their leader and listen to them and not listen to other people. I think new people come in here and they start to listen to other people outside our business who don't know anything about our company, our system, or our products; people who are extremely judgmental and prejudicial. We say that prejudice doesn't exist, but it does. There are a lot of people that are prejudiced and they discriminate. There are also people who are very opinionated and they want to give their input to a new associate, thinking that they are going to give that person some good advice. But, at the end of the day, they are giving the new associate the worst advice by telling them not to do something or to go get a job. I think that a job today is basically legalized slavery. They control your income. They control when you can go on a vacation. They control your hours. They control when you can take a break. This is, to me… Slavery, whether it was illegal or legal, I don't believe in it. I believe in free enterprise, that you do what you want to do within legal means.

I tell my associates that are new, "Listen to your coach and have only one coach, not multiple coaches. You can have multiple coaches in different areas of your life; you may have a spiritual coach, you may have a health coach, you might have a business coach and you might have somebody on a personal level that can give you guidance about marriage and life. That is fine, but when it comes to business, don't listen to other people; listen to your leadership in the business."

Common Mistakes Associates Make

One of biggest mistakes I think people make in this business is they come in here and think this is a get rich overnight type of scheme. "I'm going to make $1 million in a year or six months." Is it possible? Absolutely, it's possible to close a big deal, but I don't think, in 20 years, I've seen anybody in this business make $1 million in their first six months or year. I think that people have to understand that they need to be patient to achieve their dreams and their goals. There's an old saying that a success is not a destination, but a journey itself; it is the whole experience of getting where you are and that's number one.

I think people need to believe in themselves; most people just don't believe in themselves. They think they've got to have a high IQ or that they need college credentials; they think they need to be born on the right side of the tracks or able to talk really good; they think that they have to be really pretty and handsome and that they've got to be an active individual. None of it is true. None are necessities. Believe in yourself. Once you do, you can hang out with everybody and do anything. At the end of the day, all those people that you put on a pedestal, that you look up to, they're all just like you; they fear, they worry, they cry and they laugh. They are no different than you are. Just believe in yourself; believe that you deserve to be a champion that you deserve to be a million dollar earner.

Lack of self-worth is a mistake. You must have some self-worth. If Kobe Bryant, one of the best athletes ever, left the Los Angeles Lakers to go play on another ball club and they said, "Kobe, we are prepared to pay you $1 million a year. That's it." I wonder if Kobe would take that. I don't think he would because he knows his worth. His self-worth is $50 million, $60 million. You need to have a greater self-worth.

Another mistake people make is not following their leader. If you had a minefield and there were footprints and those footprints ended up on the other side of the field, wouldn't you step in the same footprints rather than find your own? Not doing so is just stupid. I tell people to just follow the footprints of their leader and that's it.

Also, people say, "I don't like recruiting." I think that's a mistake because everything is about recruiting, isn't it? I mean, the military recruits, churches recruit every day, big collegiate teams recruit from high schools every day. You know, there's a great movie called *The Wizard of Oz* and the main character is a girl named Dorothy. Even Dorothy, as she was trying to get to her destination, was a recruiter. She recruited three people along the way — Lion, Scarecrow and Tin Man. Each one of these people had deficiencies — one of them had no courage, one of them had no heart, one of them had no brain — but they all reached the destination, despite all the tremendous adversity they encountered, because they were a team.

Even Jesus was a great recruiter and he went 12 wide. Look at Jesus. His hierarchy today, it's huge!

My Advice To A Leader Who Is Stuck In A Rut

If you really want to get to the next level, you have to have big, big aspirations. You have to want more, to be more. The larger your aspirations, the greater your drive to complete them. Every waking moment you have to think about how to get to the next level. It must consume everything you do. It's almost an addiction to have that aspiration and to want it so badly that you can't get it out of your mind. It's like being young and in love. Young people in love will do anything to spend time with each other. It's an addictive feeling that you cannot get out of your mind. It is like I was talking about at a leadership meeting we had yesterday, I was telling my people how drug addicts who have no job; no direction in life and no money still find ways to acquire drugs. If people have no means of acquiring drugs and can still get the drugs because they are addicts, imagine if you were addicted to a greater purpose; wanting to be wealthy, wanting things for your wife or for your parents. I constantly remind myself how bad I want that and you know what's crazy? If you ever sit and fixate on something that you want, you're going to get it; as long as your thoughts and your actions are congruent. If they're not congruent you are not going to get what you want. You can't say you're going to lose 25 pounds and eat whole large pizzas, double cheeseburgers with bacon, extra sauce, and French fries each day and expect lose 25 pounds. Your actions are incongruent with your thoughts. So, I say thoughts and actions have to be congruent to get to the next level.

Things I Would Do Differently If I Had To Start Over

If I were to start all over now, I would find a leader who was somebody that I believed in, that I trusted with my life, and that I could put up on a pedestal. That would be the kind of role model that I aspired to be and I would emulate him. Unfortunately for me, my leader at the time didn't have anything my wife and I didn't already have.

Second: I would literally talk to everyone. I really discriminated in my recruitment process because I looked at some people and I sized them up. I said, "There's no chance for him," or "He is ugly," or "He can't speak English," or "Oh my God, he's obese." I discriminated against people and I was very selective of the kind of people that I wanted. Early on, I didn't really understand this business and what we were here to do. Our mission is to give everybody three things: a system, an opportunity and leadership. I think we should give everybody that opportunity to come in here and embrace the system, embrace the leadership, embrace our products and give them a chance to change their life. I am grateful that they didn't discriminate against my wife and me; that they said, "Give him a chance. Let him prove himself."

The Future

My whole life, since I was probably three years old, I wanted to be an entertainer. I think I always wanted to be an actor. Every opportunity I had when I was young and I had many, many, many opportunities because we actually had people who called my parents and said, "Your son could be an incredible Hollywood star," but my mom always prevented these people from ever talking to me. My parents even sent me away to Arizona to a boarding school so people wouldn't be able to find me. So, I was isolated from all those people and from having a chance to be a star someday. My parents just felt that that world was really corrupt and that there was a lot of drug use in that industry. So, they really did want to protect me from all that and I can see that because I can see a lot of the children today in that world that grow up and become a little bit different and have different lifestyles. So, I am grateful for that but now that I'm in that world, I think I have the character and the integrity to know how to keep all that stuff in check and still have an opportunity to get out there and be in the film world or in some sort of stand-up comedy world.

Chapter 3

Marcy Blochowiak

I grew up with a middle-income family and had a great life. My parents have been married for 49 years and they believed in me. I had a nice childhood and then, you know, life just takes it course. In high school, I was very mediocre and I always thought I was supposed to do something really big. I played soccer in high school and college, and I was always looking for what I needed to do. I knew there was something out there for me.

Soccer taught me how to compete. I really enjoyed scoring goals and being recognized; that was really good. And then, after college, I left soccer and basically I went to become a Delta flight attendant. All of a sudden, there I was with big Delta Airlines and I was like, "Gosh, everything here is great," but it's not based on performance. I was making $15,300 a year, living with five flight attendants in a three bedroom apartment and I could fly for free around the world but I was still broke when I got there. So, I thought: *Well, I love Delta but it would be great if I can make some extra money.*

I really have to give my mother a lot of the credit. She grew up dirt poor in Oklahoma, always on the wrong side of the tracks. My mom was a teacher, my dad was a tailor, and when I was a young child my mom kept trying things. She did the Avon door-to-door, then she upgraded to Mary Kay. Basically, she was always looking for something to do. Then, she got into financial services and all of a sudden our lives, our lifestyle started changing. I was like, "I don't know what's going on here but something is different. Financially, things are not so taut, not so tight." My mother started in this industry and she was a great mentor for me.

Well, there I was at Delta Airlines and I got a call from my mom and she said, "Honey, I want you to come take a look at what I did." And I said, "Mom, I know what you do and I don't want to do that." I had no desire to be in the financial services. She said, "Honey, do you want me to continue to lend you money?" and I said, "Yes, Mom." My big fear was I was being threatened with being cut off financially by my mother. So, I showed up to the meeting. I showed up to the meeting and all of a sudden the "What-ifs?" began running through my mind. *What if I can make an extra $500 a month? What if I can supplement my income?* All of a sudden, it was like a whole new world opened up for me.

So, I started off very unsure, very slow but my mother kept pushing me. I think, if she had been a weak coach for me, I probably wouldn't be in the business today, but she kept saying,

CHAPTER 3
MARCY BLOCHOWIAK

"Talk to this person. You need to do this. You need to do that," and she just kept pushing me. I got so mad at her because she pushed me so hard. Then I started growing, I started doing appointments by myself, recruiting people, and making sales. Within a short period, I was making more money part-time than I was making full-time at Delta… and I fired Delta Airlines back in 1994.

Soon after I started, I met my incredible husband through the company. I got a marriage and a merger 18 years ago and then the good Lord blessed us with our only child almost six years ago. And I'll tell you what: It's been an incredible life. It has not been easy, but it's been simple and it's absolutely been worth it.

Starting Out Single In The Business

What I realized when I first got started in the business was that I didn't know much about the financial side but I knew I was supposed to recruit. I thought: *I don't know how the financial thing works but I can talk to people.* So, there I was, single and I still had a lot of guy friends. I started inviting them to presentations… but I had learned that I shouldn't invite them to the office but rather to meet them at a third location.

So, there was this steak restaurant about a half a mile from our office and one night — and usually not everybody you invite shows up — I had three guys show up in the parking lot and — this is no joke: One got out of his car and he had a bouquet of flowers. Another guy got out of the car and he had a bottle of wine. The third guy got out of the car too…and they all showed up at the same time and they all saw each other at the same time. They were not really happy following me in their cars to the BPM, but some of them signed up, some of them became clients and some of them never talked to me again. That's okay.

Meeting My Spouse In The Business

We were in Atlanta and the company was just getting started. There weren't more than a few hundred people at this conference. So, I was just checking the whole thing out and I saw this tall, handsome guy walk across stage to give what would be called the Senior Marketing Director promotion in today's world. I thought: *Gosh I don't know who he is but I sure would like to meet him.* So, the next time at that conference, I made sure I was sitting close to him and when they were passing out papers, I passed the paper to him and kind of took it back. We started getting to know each other at that conference. I asked him how old he was and I realized he was three and a half years younger than me. He looked at me with this look on his face like, "Gosh. How old is this lady?" So, at that point, he did not get my phone number and I was like, "Oh man. I could have handled that differently." But then, a few weeks later, I got a call from him and he told me he'd looked me up in information. He challenged me to a recruiting contest. I beat him that month in recruiting and he sent me flowers. We started dating long distance after that.

What Are The Keys To My Personal Success?

I think there are a few things. I paid attention to leaders in the company that were winning in business. I read a lot. Also, I surrounded myself with really good people. I'm always around people that are positive and uplifting who don't have a lot of negativity or drama. I also had a really good work ethic. I was one of those crazy people who was very coachable. So, if I was asked to do something by someone I respected, I really tried to do it.

I think I developed really good relationships with people. Anytime I brought someone in the business, they knew that I was a friend for them first. I always found what was nice and important to them and I tried to help them hit their goals.

My Advice To A New Associate

I'd give them a few things. The first thing I'd really want to know is what drives them. I would want to know what moves them emotionally — so much so that, when they think about it, they get misty-eyed. If I can find that out in someone, I can gear this business around that and then I can really help them to become unstoppable.

The second thing is that I make sure that we fast-start them. My goal, when I get with them, is that, immediately, they have someone come to the presentation or that we have a field training appointment. My goal is for them see the result right away.

My Advice To A Leader Who Is Stuck In A Rut

I think that they need to get back to the basics. They need to identify their "whys" again because they need to have something that drives them. They need to come up with a new top 25 list. I'm going to steal something I learned from another great leader: They've got to beat their best personal effort a year ago; they've always got to be doing better.

Things I Would Do Differently If I Had To Start Over

I would do a lot of things differently but the thing that comes to mind the most is that I would be better at creating independent people. Point in case: When we had our daughter and I took a little break from the business, we had a lot of people leave. It was a big wake-up call for me because I realized that I had created dependent people, not independent people.

So, I've learned a lot from that. My team is always going to know I believe in them but now I'm giving them a chance to get their knees scraped, to fall off the bike, to have things happen so that they can grow as people and not try to do it for them as much as I did in the past.

CHAPTER3
MARCYBLOCHOWIAK

Chapter 4
Jeff Blochowiak

The last job I had before this business was loading boxes in trucks. I would stay up late watching TV commercials selling real estate success systems and dream of a better life. Around that time, I stopped by a friend's office while he was in a meeting with a very enthusiastic man named Greg Kapp. I invited myself into the conversation and ended up being invited to a business presentation meeting. I found a system, a cause, and a coach! Greg pushed me through my shyness and, a year later, I had a full-time income and a dream business. I also moved out of my parents' basement and bought a new car!

Meeting My Spouse In The Business

Greg invited me to a big meeting that was taking place in Atlanta. I had no idea how that meeting was about to change my life, and it did in more ways than one. Marcy sat next to me at the event and we started having a conversation. She started interviewing me: "What are your recruiting numbers?" she asked. "How old are you?" So, I wondered: *How old is she?* When I told her how old I was, she said, "You're just a baby." I didn't really like the way she said that. I said, "Maybe I'll see you at the next meeting."

I went back to Milwaukee and I wished I had asked for her business card or phone number. So, I called information, got her number, and I called her. I challenged her to a recruiting contest. She beat me by one recruit! I sent her flowers and we started a long distance relationship. She was working at an airline, so she could fly for free.

After a year, she quit the airline. No more free flight benefits! The next day, I bought a ring and that's how I ended up in Atlanta. We had a marriage and a merger. I moved to Atlanta in 1996 and it's been a great partnership for us. There is nothing like dreaming and creating a future together. We have a true partnership in raising our daughter, Sophia, and building a business.

What Are The Keys To My Personal Success?

There are two key ingredients to my success. One is a commitment to personal growth. I had great mentors that always encouraged me to read books. I was always listening to audios of success — both inside of our company and outside of it. If you condition your mind to the right thinking and you just keep putting good stuff in, you're going to start having different mental habits. That will lead to great habits in your life and in your business. The person that we are when we start isn't the person that's going to cause us to win. So, having a commitment to personal growth is everything.

The second key ingredient for me is having a passion for our mission and helping people financially. I wanted to learn everything I could about the concepts, the tools and the services that we could deliver to help people. I became very confident about how I could really go out there and make a difference. I think we become very convincing once we are convinced ourselves. I had no doubt I could help people. I started to get the results; once you're getting results and making money, it's a lot easier to recruit and build a business. Making money came as a result of really having a passion for the mission and learning how to help people with our services.

My Advice To A New Associate

The biggest advice that I would give to a new associate is to not care so much about what people think. That's the one thing that always would hold me back — worrying about what someone would think about my business or think about me. That would hold me back on prospecting and phone calls. I was naturally very shy when I started in the business. I found that shy equals broke; less shy, less broke; and no shy, no broke. I got over my shyness when I started worrying less about what people thought and caring more about them.

Another piece of advice for a new associate would be to stay coachable and to stay aligned. There's a shortcut to success: Do it right the first time! There are many successful people in our company and when you have a successful mentor, you can be accountable to them and be coached. That is the shortcut to success that's available in our company.

My mentors taught me to take responsibility for the growth and momentum of my business by building legs deep. Everything good that has happened in my business career has come from following that advice. It's easy to forget; it's easy to get caught up in the day-to-day and not focus on continually driving legs deep. I was taught work from the bottom of your base legs. That creates the magic of our business.

Experience is what causes us to win big. In order to get that experience, sometimes we get beat up along the way. When we let go of the baggage that we have acquired at that point in our career, we can take advantage of the experience. Many leaders start beating themselves up and say, "I should be further along," or "I should be doing as good as that person." They forget that they are closer to success than they ever have been. They have so much experience, they know so much and they're the best leader they've ever been. When we can let go of the baggage and take all the experience that we have, we can restart our business from there and have a chance to do what any of the big leaders have done.

Things I Would Do Differently If I Had To Start Over

If I were to start all over again, I would remember to never stop prospecting and personally recruiting. When we recruit a team for the first time, start making some money or hit a promotion, it's easy to forget what got us there. We tend to slow down the habits that made us win. The temptation is to get into the management trap. The moment you think you have a team, you better get a new one fast. It's when you really do have a team that is when your example counts most.

Chapter 5

Michael Stokes

I am the youngest of four. My mother was a schoolteacher and my father was a Princeton graduate, corporate type guy. He'd always tell all his kids, "Go get a good college education and a good solid job. Work for a solid company and they will take care of you." We all followed that advice.

I wasn't the greatest student, but was able to make it into college. After college, I started working in the pharmaceutical industry. I worked for Pfizer selling drugs, legally of course. I was there for about four years and was on a fixed income, making $3,500 per month. My wife, Stacey, was in the recruiting business, making $3,000 per month. There was an opening for a promotion in a new territory for the company and I was passed over. At Pfizer, it was a very political environment and you got promoted based on who you knew, not your performance.

I starting looking at different types of businesses and other sources of income, to make ends meet. I tried different types of network marketing businesses, like Amway. There are great people in those organizations. However, the products were somewhat limited and I just really couldn't make any money to free myself from my corporate job.

An uncle of mine called and asked me if I was interested in making some additional income. I said, "Sure. What is it?" He said, "It will be about an hour. Come down to the meeting and check it out," and I said, "Here we go again… another one of those network marketing companies?" So I asked him, "Really, what is it?" He said it was a financial services company, it was expanding and it was looking for people. My first thought was: *I know nothing about finances.* The only thing I knew about finances was that money went through my checkbook faster than it went in. We were living paycheck to paycheck at the time and so, I was intrigued. Even when I went to the meeting, I knew my credit card wouldn't work so they couldn't get any money from me. I really had nothing to lose.

I sat through the presentation and it was very interesting. It talked about saving money, which we hadn't done any of; talked about getting out of debt, which I had lots of; but, what intrigued me was the opportunity to make additional income. The presenter said if I did four plans per month, I could make $3,500 per month. I didn't even know what the four plans were that they were talking about. My thought was: If they were willing to hire me and teach me how to do those four plans, I could double my income and my wife could stop working and be a stay-at-home mother, which was a goal of ours.

In 10 months part-time, I made more money than I was making full-time. Actually, in my 10th month, I made $4,000 and I fired my boss.

What Are The Keys To My Personal Success?

Certainly, there are so many different keys to success. The number one thing is: You've got to lead by example. In anything, whether you're going to be a good parent, be a good business owner, you have to lead by example. You have to do what you say you're going to do. If you're going to have other people do what you're doing then you have to do it yourself and show them how to do it. So many times, I have seen managers that would tell other people to do things that they weren't willing to do themselves.

The second key is self-development. Until I started with WFG, I had never been exposed to any form of self-development. My mentor told me to start reading books on leadership and success. He said we "become" the people we hang around and the books we read. The two most important books were *Think and Grow Rich and How To Win friends & Influence People.*

Third is a strong work ethic. Working nine to five is for survival, it always has been. With our business model, you can multiply your time and efforts through many people. That's the key to wealth and security.

My Advice To A New Associate

When I got started in the business, my focus was on sales not recruiting, because that was my background. My advice would be to focus on recruiting. The sales will come. You need to be coachable and follow the system.

When I think about when I got started, there was another leader at the time that had done extremely well in the business. One of the top guys in the business had no experience in sales at all, but he focused on recruiting. Today, he has a multimillion dollar business. If I would have changed anything, I would have been totally sold out and focused 1000% to recruiting from the start.

My Advice To A Leader Who Is Stuck In A Rut

They need to refocus on the reasons why they started the business; start fresh one more time. Go back to when you first started—the excitement and how you felt about all the possibilities. Gain back that motivation. A lot of times, we get comfortable with our situation. In this business, you can make some really good money and have a really comfortable lifestyle. However, that comfort level is also the greatest enemy and can prevent you from taking it to the next level and be great.

Secondly, always have the end in mind. So many of us have an SMD, EMD or CEO slump. We hit the goal and don't realize that it wasn't as great as we thought it was. We kind of idolize the title, think we made it, and get comfortable again. We need to keep focused on our next goal, ahead of time, as we're going for the current one. Always stay hungry, for yourself and your team. For our team, our challenge was to hit CEO. Once we hit it, we thought, "This is it." We didn't have everything in place or the mindset in place to go to EVC. We are now getting back and retooling to make that happen. That's the great thing about the business. You can always restart and, in six months, hit your next big promotion.

Third, you, as the leader, need to lead by example. You have to be the change agent. The leader has to be the person who goes in there and makes the change. It's not going to happen with you telling everybody to do what you're not doing. You need to rally your team to do the same. I think the best way to motivate somebody is find out their reasons why and remind them of those reason why when they're getting their emotional cans kicked.

Things I Would Do Differently If I Had To Start Over

I would have taken the business a lot more seriously because now I know what we have to offer. Sometimes, we get involved in things we just want to try and see if they work and if they do, great. If they don't, we don't either. If people really understood what they had here and what the possibilities are, I think they would be a lot more focused and work a lot harder.

Second, as I said before, be a lot more focused on recruiting because it really is the key to our business. Although we get paid on the sales, I think a lot of people don't realize that it's not the sales, recruiting is a means to an end and so we need to be focused on the recruiting.

Third thing would be I'd probably have a little bit more financial discipline. That's the business that we're in and I think it's important that we have that.

CHAPTERS
MICHAEL STOKES

Chapter 6
Marla Isidro

I was one of the lucky ones who grew up in a business environment. My parents are both business owners. My uncles and aunts are all business owners. I didn't know anybody who worked for somebody else. I grew up with my parents saying, "You've got to work for yourself, don't ever work for anyone, don't farm anyone else's land." I'm one of the lucky ones... but coming here to America was a totally different story.

We moved from the Philippines to start a new life, because we maxed out what the Philippines could offer. My husband and I were only in our late 20s. We had so much more to give but we wanted bigger opportunities hence, a bigger legacy for our growing family. Therefore, we moved to America because it's the land of the free, the land of opportunities. Other countries don't give the same opportunity. The downside is that, as soon as we landed, instead of finding a business opportunity, they said we had to have a permit to work.

My husband was an engineer and I was an accountant, a CPA, back in the Philippines. I became a CPA so I could account for my own business. I asked, "How do you get permission to work?" They said I could work as an accountant. I thought they meant I could run my own business as an accountant, but they said, "No, you have to work as an accountant." So, I had to start over and work for somebody else. I was a lousy employee, but I was lucky to have a good CPA boss as a mentor. I moved on to work as a senior accountant for the biggest shopping mall in the country. There, I was exposed to commercial real estate and leasing, but that required too much money to get started on that scale.

My husband, Lito and I were looking for a way to start a business and we decided to open a water store, because it was the only thing we could afford. The neighborhood store we were getting our water from, was for sale. We had our green cards, so we could start over with a new opportunity. I worked five days a week as an accountant and then, on weekends, I worked at the store. So, I really worked seven days a week and carried those five gallon water containers by myself out to people's trunks.

One day, a man walked in and asked if we delivered water. We had no license for deliveries, but I said, "Yes," anyway. He gave me his card. His real estate and mortgage office was only a block away. I had been thinking about going into the loan industry because in 2005; everybody wanted to be a loan officer and I wanted to make more money. I offered him free water and told him that I was an accountant too and I was willing to do that for free, if taught me how to be a loan officer and do mortgages. He said, "Sure. What are you doing Tuesday night?" The man was Oscar Menjivar and he happened to be John Shin's partner and working in real estate, but he actually was doing WFG.

I went on Tuesday night and saw John Shin. I thought he was Chinese and didn't really listen to what he was saying, because I was waiting for a real estate presentation that never happened. I did hear him talk about WFG. Two or three weeks later, he followed up with me and asked me, "Where are you at?" He told me there was a big event happening at the Marriott in Woodland Hills, right where I lived, and that I should go. I thought I was finally going to hear about real estate, but it was John Shin again. I was sitting in the back thinking: *I left my kids at home and this is what I get again. I'm going to kill Oscar... but he's my client, so I have to keep him.* I didn't hear the whole presentation because I was just mad that it was the same as before, even though I didn't really hear it the first time. You have the idea: the same things, the same jokes. John even talked about being a lawyer. He talked about his SAT scores and what a loser he was. I thought: *Why am I listening to this guy?* I really didn't get it. At the end of the talk, John Shin said, "There's a lady, she's been around just two weeks and her background is in entertainment. She does a little bit of acting on the side here and there, and she waits on tables while she's waiting for her big break. She's been around only two weeks and is on her way to make over $100,000." That woke me up. If she could do it, not having any business background, then so could I.

I still didn't get started with WFG, but this guy was persistent. Maybe it was fate, because everywhere I went, I saw him. I would see him coming and I wanted to get out of the way. I would hope he hadn't seen me, but he would catch me every time. I thought it was fate that kept him knocking at my door.

Then I went and signed up, but I really didn't get it. I told Lito,

"I think they do a little bit of this and they do a little bit of that," and then he said, "Why don't you try it?" I asked if he would let me. My husband didn't really stay at home. He was a truck driver at that time and he only was home once every two months. So, I was a single mom most of the time. I had the water business and I had two boys on top of Lito, so that's three boys. It worked, the company is amazing, and I love telling the story of how I started.

What Are The Keys To My Personal Success?

Determination and discipline are my keys. I wanted to really make my mom proud. Why? My mom said, "You've got to conquer America. You already maxed out other things. Where are you going to go?" I think it was more of where to go from there. Personal success is more about looking back and saying, "Do I really want to go backwards?"

I was determined to go forward and make myself a success. Discipline is something my parents raised me with. I remember a story where my mom adhered to high standards, so much that it was close to abuse. It's what helped me be successful, but if it was with anybody who was an employee, who had a low mental attitude, they would really think it was abuse. I remember how she got me to learn spelling. At our grocery store, I would do the inventory of the Angus beef from Australia. I did the count once, and I wrote "150 pieces of stake." I don't remember how old I was, maybe 11 or 12, but my mom put it out there by the fridge where the steaks were sold. The following day, I came in and I saw how I misspelled it. I was so embarrassed that she hung it out there and did not just tell me it was misspelled. My mom only finished 5th grade, but she wanted to be a lawyer so she always tried to better herself. She could not speak English well, but she knew her vocabulary. I know she put it out there to embarrass me. I knew all of her customers who knew how to spell knew I wrote it and that I misspelled it.

I'd rather have a coach tell me the truth, than lie to me. When John says I'm doing great, even if I know I'm not, I get mad at him. I tell him, "You know what? I'm not going to get to the next level, if you tell me exactly what you told that other lady. I know you told her what she wanted to hear." I don't want to hear that you love me, even if I'm not doing well. You tell me the truth, like my mom did, and that's why I'm here. I think personal success is about discipline, determination and everyone adhering to a higher standard.

My Advice To A New Associate

I would tell them to put on blinders to get them to their goal without distractions. When I started here, I did not look at what anybody else was doing. I didn't see any distractions, I had blinders on. Everybody laughed at me and said, "If John says jump, you will." They laughed at me for following John too much. I even answered them, "Yeah, if John says jump, I'll ask how high. If he asks me to eat kimchi, maybe I won't, but I will act like I did. I would probably try it, if he says it's going to make me successful." What if my mom didn't guide me, how did we know the right food to eat? It's the same with this company. I look at it the same way I was raised.

If they wear blinders, they don't have a chance to look around and get distracted. They must really trust that their leaders are going to get them to the promised land. Otherwise, every time they open their eyes without blinders, they will see the hurdles. Imagine if hurdlers looked at a hurdle and then just stopped; instead, they just jump whenever they see a hurdle.

I'd rather John say, "Right, left, straight then right," and I go right and then fall in a hole and get back up. If he says again, "Go right because you missed a hole." Trust your leadership because they've been there and they have your best interest at heart. Trust that they're going to get you to the next level.

My Advice To A Leader Who Is Stuck In A Rut

They should do the same thing that got them to where they are now. Showing a great example is better than asking somebody to do it. If they got where they are by personally producing, personally field training and personally making calls, that's what they should be doing. Just do it over and over again because practice makes perfect. What's great about this business is that doing things the right way isn't necessarily the key. Putting a massive amount of people in front of this business is what will make you successful.

Things I Would Do Differently If I Had To Start Over

I would not stop trying to be number one. I would not stop at $300,000 annual income. I would not stop helping myself. I think that John was right, coaches are always right. He didn't want to mentor me in the beginning because my goal was only to make $10,000 a month to retire Lito. So, John suspected I was going to stop when I got there, but I didn't. When I tripled that, I did stop, without even realizing it. I think I missed the higher law where you don't stop helping other people. You know how they say, "Put the mask on yourself and then put it on the next person?"

On an airplane, I put the mask on myself and didn't look to see if somebody else needed one. The person next to me was dying, but I was thinking, "Oh, I'm good. Good luck to you." When somebody needs help, we should not be looking at how far we've come, but at how many people we can bring to where we are now. That's the beauty of the business: We can really bring people to a higher level.

The Future

I'm excited to see myself at the next level and doing it one more time. I'm excited about that question and that challenge; that makes me get up right now and go. I'm excited anytime I see something that has not been done before. John says, "This number hasn't been done before," and I will go do it. I'm excited about how big this opportunity is and I know there is no limit. I'm excited about maximizing it and seeing how far I can go with it and not stopping until I drop.

CHAPTER6
MARLA ISIDRO

Chapter 7

Hanna Horenstein

My life began in Toronto, Canada, but I moved to California at eight years old; the vast majority of my experiences and memories take place in the U.S. I was fortunate that my parents always understood and taught the need for entrepreneurship, especially the benefits of owning your own businesses. Even though they didn't always succeed in each and every venture they began, they continued to reinvent themselves. These concepts were instilled in me early and often and became a major part of my life.

My father grew a business as a real estate developer and owned his own Real Estate company, while my mother stayed at home with my sister and me. Once she and I were old enough to fend for ourselves, my mom began working with my dad in his real estate business. This eventually fueled her own entrepreneurship, building a medium-sized clothing company. It wasn't until much later in my career that my mom would join me in my business and again achieved entrepreneurial success.

This culture of entrepreneurship in the home helped develop my own entrepreneurial ambitions. My desire to establish and grow my own business started with getting my real estate license immediately upon turning eighteen, the earliest opportunity for obtaining that license. While building my real estate business, I identified the need for realtors to have a marketing service that allowed for more exposure for their listings. This lead to my establishment of a real estate marketing company. Although my partner and I bowed out of the real estate marketing arena after only one year, the experience of developing and running that company heavily contributed to my desire to create a business of my own that could take on a life of its own.

My next adventure into business ownership arose out of a short-term introduction to the mortgage industry. While working in mortgages, I realized the benefits of the "broker" position. Brokers earn their income from both the efforts of their own work and the work of others, rather than the mortgage loan officer, who only earns income from their own efforts. While earning good commissions through the mortgage company, I was having multiple conversations with my friend, Jamie Villalovos, about her future. She was working at Bally's Fitness, but was very unhappy with her job, completely lacking any direction in her career, but trying to get into the real estate or mortgage business after passing her licensing exam. I was able to help her get a position with my mortgage company, but after only one month, she left the mortgage business. Her quick departure really piqued my interest in what she was doing, especially when she refused to give me any information about it.

It wasn't until I was visiting her at her house that I saw a box on her kitchen table with "WMA" printed on it. I questioned her further about what she had gotten involved in and she refused to give me any information, but she invited me to a presentation at her new office and an interview with John Shin. I was impressed with the information presented in that meeting and immediately realized the importance of the information I received; I joined that day. That decision has caused the greatest impact in my life, allowing me to realize my potential as a person who can inspire others to achieve their potential. These efforts are the pinnacle of my entrepreneurship and WFG has taught me, and allowed me, to achieve it.

What Are The Keys To My Personal Success?

Success is almost always built on a foundation of numerous "keys." One of those "keys" for me has always been persistence. My persistence came from a strong desire to achieve. Not just to achieve something, but to achieve something bigger than myself, something that allowed me to raise others up.

Without persistence, I could never achieve anything. I had to set my mind to a goal, and then make concerted efforts to achieve it. I learned early on that hearing "no," or getting turned down, meant that I needed to learn why and approach the problem from a different angle to overcome the hurdle. Persistence, in and of itself, however, is not enough. It is just like the old saying: "insanity is doing the same thing over and over again and expecting different results." It is through the combination of persistence and introspection that I attain my goals and my greatest achievements.

Each of my promotions and successes came as a result of this marriage of persistence and introspection. In each case, I made a decision to reach one of my goals, and was unwavering in my efforts to get it done. Regardless of whether I was encouraged or discouraged in those efforts, whether it was "unrealistic" or within my grasp, my persistence allowed me to overcome the obstacles keeping me from my goals. When I was told "no," it didn't mean "no" to me; it meant "not right now" or "not this way." Each time, I realized that I needed to understand the hurdle or the objection and find ways to overcome the obstacles; each time I would follow up, remember my previous mistakes (of which there were many), and exercise patience. Sometimes it took six months, sometimes 6 days, and sometimes 6 years (all depending on the goal I was working towards). In every reasonable case (and many unreasonable cases) my introspective persistence got me through and allowed me to attain my goals.

Persistence requires the right mindset. I've read hundreds of books throughout the last 20 years on personal development, success, and improvement. Individual growth is imperative to continued personal improvement. I think most people make the mistake of stopping that process; their goals become plateaus rather than platforms from which to move upward. By continuing personal development - especially by working with coaches and mentors, by seeking out leadership, and by always looking for the next step - continued success is achievable.

My Advice To A New Associate

Almost every associate has the ability to succeed. Although success doesn't come easily, new associates need to believe in themselves. If an associate dedicates themselves to success, they will succeed. One of the mistakes that I made early on was taking a long time before believing in myself and the process, and actually taking the steps necessary to start my business, such as getting licensed.

I had to go through a process of making that decision. It took me six months to apply for my license, and then another six months to complete the licensing process. This year-long effort could have been shortened to a few months had I allowed myself to believe. If I had believed from the beginning, I would have gone "all-in" and thrown myself into building my company nine months earlier. Stop being skeptical; if you have decided to do it, then do it.

Next, be careful from whom you take advice. Everyone has an opinion and everyone has an opinion on what you should and shouldn't be doing. Once the decision has been made to achieve, look to those who have achieved before for your advice and counsel. Usually that means looking to those who have achieved success within the particular business, to which you have dedicated yourself to, to get your answers. If you look to get approval from people outside your chosen business, you are not going to get it.

Fortunately, early on, I made sure my advice came from the leaders in my company; I made sure that I qualified for all of the trips and I attended all of the events put on by the company. I associated with those leaders that had achieved what I wanted to achieve; and I took the time to ask them how they got to where they are, what their challenges were and what advice they could give me. I took advice from those who achieved before me, not the skeptics. There are too many skeptics and their skepticism will fuel your own; it will give you justifications to quit any meaningful business.

My Advice To A Leader Who Is Stuck In A Rut

As I said before, most "ruts" are not really "ruts," but plateaus on which otherwise successful people have allowed themselves to land. The difference between a "plateau" and a "platform" is that platforms provide you access to the next level. However, any "plateau" can become a "platform" merely through the mind-set of the leader. Dedication, perseverance and persistence provide the "ladder" to move to the next level.

Approximately five years ago, my husband David joined me in the business. Together, we have accelerated our business and are working toward our ultimate goal of becoming EVC's. However, David and I had been stuck at EMD for a long while. Our "ladder" was forged from a dedicated effort to discuss and decide on our goals. We wrote out a new business plan and made a decision to go to CEO. We studied the guidelines but they seemed impossible. We needed to promote out three SMDs and do what seemed like an unachievable amount of production; more than we had ever done in such a short period of time. Before committing ourselves to this goal, we consulted with Jamie and Shawn Villalovos, leaders we respected and who had achieved the levels we were looking to achieve. We discussed the numbers with Jaime and she gave us hope. She encouraged us to achieve these successes. After all, she had achieved them in very similar circumstances and was confident that we could, too.

After dedicating ourselves to achieving CEO, we analyzed what needed to be done by working backwards. We looked at exactly what needed to get done, and we engaged our entire team to achieve the promotions they needed. We knew that by encouraging, uplifting, and pushing others to achieve (rather than focusing on our own needs), regardless of whether or not they believed they could get promoted, we would achieve our own goals. The same thing is true with clients: by ensuring we are doing the right thing for our clients, we will get sales.

It worked. By focusing on our belief in our people and their potential, we achieved our own promotion. We got them engaged, we held them accountable, and we spoke to them every single day. We put up banners on the wall, we talked about it at every single meeting, we did conference calls, we tracked all the business, and we tracked all the numbers.

We raised our people up and at the same time, got them to commit to helping us. These efforts encouraged others. All of a sudden, people were coming out of nowhere saying, "I have this 401K that I need to roll over. Can you do that for me?" or "I think I need to get another life insurance policy." If I can contribute to the run, let's go ahead and do that right now." It was a team effort. It was only through that team effort that we were ever able to achieve our goals.

Those who have reached their "plateau" are usually focusing on their day to day lives; they have not identified and dedicated themselves to a particular goal. By identifying the goal; dedicating yourself to achieving that goal; energizing, helping, and promoting your team; focusing them on a common goal and each person's role within that goal; you will motivate your people and allow them to help you, coming out of nowhere to achieve your goals.

Things I Would Do Differently If I Had To Start Over

The most important trait an individual can have when they are starting this business is to be "coachable." I was not coachable when I began, and I see people every day who limit their achievement by not allowing themselves to use the knowledge and experience of others to overcome hurdles that have already been overcome. I thought I knew it all and I wanted to do things my way. I thought I could come up with a better way to do things. Reinventing the wheel doesn't work, especially in this business. Instead, by following the system already in place, an individual can succeed and achieve great successes.

Being coachable allows me, or others, to work smarter and not necessarily as hard. As I said, most hurdles have already been experienced and overcome. By releasing your skepticism and leveraging your leadership for their knowledge and mentorship, you are working smarter. Those new to the business usually don't understand or recognize these opportunities. However, it is also the best time to take advantage because everyone wants to help you. Your leadership will help by making appointments for you, go on appointments with you, and recruit with you. By taking advantage of this critical time, a new associate can raise his business from day one.

In addition to coachability, I would allow my leaders and mentors to make me move forward faster. By releasing my skepticism, dedicating myself to achievement, clearly identifying my goals, and creating a complete business plan, my mentors and leadership would have been able to put my business into "warp speed" and help me achieve greater results. With the business environment and planning available today, associates can come in and achieve CEO within their first three years, as long as they allow themselves to take advantage of the resources available to them.

The Future

The future is exciting, and especially in what I see for my team. We have some incredible leaders developing on our team. David and I are watching people that we brought in the business years ago, that came from completely different fields, come in financially destitute. We did their financial plans when they first came in. They had nothing saved and they were making very little money. Now, we are watching them buy their own homes, open their own offices and explode their incomes. We are also seeing them promote out their own leaders. This allows us to love what we do for families, both through financial planning and through association with our company. While I get excited about both parts, what made me fall in love with this business is watching the lives of our associates change and improve through their affiliation with this business.

Another exciting part of our business is seeing it take on a life of its own. We are seeing where others can go in the next couple of years and we have a whole new energy right now and a whole new mindset.

My Dream

My dream is a life which allows me to make my own schedule, spend time with my family when and where I want to, plan vacations where and when I want to, and create true financial independence. I can spend time with my kids — have the fun times, taking them out, taking them to Disneyland and Chucky Cheese when we feel like it. We are planning some vacations right now that are going to be absolutely incredible, including taking our kids to Hawaii every single year. This business gets me closer to that dream every month.

Our daughter is going to be four in December, and the next Hawaii trip she takes in February will be her fifth time in Hawaii; our son will be two and this will be his third trip. It has become something that they look forward to every year, and it is exciting to share that with them. The memories we create on these vacations are irreplaceable. And this company has allowed me and my family to together create those memories in just fourteen years.

For most people, they have worked at a job for fourteen years and received paychecks. They've paid their bills — and that's great — but they haven't built anything of long-term value. We have something. We have residual income, a business, a team, incredible friends, mentors, and a lifestyle. Fortunately, I was able to get in the business early and dedicate myself to my own success, and with a company that allows for that success. For that, I am very grateful.

CHAPTER7
HANNAHORENSTEIN

Chapter 8
Randy Sicairos

I was actually introduced to the company by my father. At that time, we were going through some tremendous financial difficulties. My dad was a truck driver for many years and my mom was actually a caregiver. I saw them work hard their whole life. They came here from a different country. I grew up on a little farm in Watsonville, California and I learned to work hard every single day. We had work to do before we went to school every single day and that taught me how to work hard. My mom would always tell me that I could be the President of the United States one day if I wanted to and I could do anything that I put my mind to, but I never had found an environment where I could succeed or challenge myself other than the soccer field.

My father was always looking for a business and had started different businesses, but failed, which caused arguments at home. I remember, for some parts of my childhood more than others, my parents arguing over the lack of money and constantly living under financial pressure. Somehow, my parents always managed to make us feel like there was plenty to go around. It's only now that I have a family of my own that I can look back and only imagine the stress they faced. Somehow, they always endured with a smile. All that my brother and I could see was two loving parents that worked hard for what we had, but I was nosey enough to know Mom and Dad were under a lot of pressure, which mounted as time went on.

It's truly my parents' example of drive and thirst for a better life that inspires me, to this day, to change the course for our family and fight for a better life. It was their dream for a better life that led them to this country from Mexico.

When I started the business, it was because my brother got involved in a bad motorcycle accident. He was in a coma for two months and hospitalized for about a year and that came along with a $720,000 medical bill. At that time, I was 19 years old. My parents had just begun the process of a separation and things weren't positive at home, but my brother was going through this challenge. So, the family came together and my dad got me in this business because he felt this would be an opportunity for me to do something. I was in Europe, trying to achieve a professional soccer career and it didn't work out. So, I came back and said, "Okay. I guess I'll go to school like everyone else." Once I went and sat down with the counselors to weigh my options, I knew that I didn't want to go to school. So, my dad found this business and forced me to do the business. I didn't want to do it at all and he made me do it and I'm very glad that he did.

My parents were clients and Eric did a home presentation at my parents' house. I was sitting in the kitchen, not even a part of the presentation, but I heard what he was talking about and, little by little, I got closer and closer to the presentation. Out of 42 people in that home presentation, I was the only person that got recruited. There were six clients and one recruit, that one recruit was me. Shortly after that, my up line quit and then, from there, I was direct to Eric under his mentorship. He had heard about some of the challenges I was having. So, he called and offered to move me into his house and he mentored me for a year and a half. He told me that I didn't have to pay rent for the first few months; all I had to do was go to church with him on Sunday and work hard. I knew I was in the right place and then, from there, I just kept fighting. I was 19 years old and just wanted to get better and better and prove that I could make it here.

What Are The Keys To My Personal Success?

I would say that success is something that you need to want constantly. You need to want to be successful. I think that you need to have a burning desire to want to be more and that desire makes you do all the work that it takes to be successful. Whether you need to personally develop yourself or just to get to work to stop being lazy. The reasons why you want to be successful and you having that burning desire in yourself is what makes you do whatever it takes to be successful. It takes different things for different people, depending on where you come from or where you are in life. Your burning desire and your dedication to wanting to get there is what will eventually take you there and keep that desire alive.

My Advice To A New Associate

For a new person, just getting started, one thing I would say is to accept that you will have to change for your life to change. You will have to change to be able to do something you've never done before. So, accept change to be a part of your life and know that the person you are now, is not the one that's going to make you successful; understand that it's nothing personal or anything that has to do with anything other than you being successful and being willing to change.

Also, I would say that you have to believe that you can do this business. So, believe and really understand that you can get there and that there is a very simple system, mentors, and leadership in place. Everything's in place for you to do it. You just have to believe it and see yourself there and back it up at work.

Challenges Of Starting At A Young Age

For someone young and getting started in this business, I think you have to accept the fact that you cannot act young. You can be young, but cannot act young. I started this business when I was 19. Eric told me I had to act like I was 40, married with kids; that if I could act 40, married with kids then I would attract the right people and I would have a chance at being successful. You need to hold yourself to a different standard.

I only associated with people that were older than me. I let go of all my old friends. Whoever was not willing to come with me, I left them behind. I knew there were bigger things out there for me. Not only did I start associating with older people, but I also started modeling them. I accepted that if I was going to be successful, I had to model what successful people do.

My Advice To A Leader Who Is Stuck In A Rut

I would say that you have to come to a point where you are dissatisfied enough to do something about it. There are a lot of people who are frustrated or comfortable. Those could all be symptoms, but eventually that has to turn into something; you have to get frustrated enough to go do something about it. Attack this business from a different angle. Get congruent with your leadership. There's no substitute for alignment, mentorship, and someone guiding you along the way. There's no substitute for that but I think that what causes people to reach out is that they're so frustrated, they're finally willing to do something about it and what you find is that the same thing that you have to do is the same thing that you were told to do from the very beginning.

My mom told me to always do things right the first time so I didn't have to do it twice. I think, for frustrated leaders that are not where they want to be, if they could just go back and just say, "I'm going to do everything that my leader tells me to do, regardless of the price," I think the reward would come a lot faster.

Also, getting reignited by why you started this business in the first place is important. I started here to retire my parents and to give a great example for my brother. That was my initial thing and we were able to do that. Now, I want to go out and make a difference in the world and inspire other people to do the same thing that was possible for me.

Things I Would Do Differently If I Had To Start Over

If I were to start over, one thing I would do different is talk to the people that I'm scared to talk to. For many years, I would talk to people who were young. They were easier to talk to. I knew I could influence them much easier than someone who was in their 40s and 50s, but I got nowhere talking to people that didn't bring much to the table in business.

Once, I remember being so frustrated in my business and I remember I found a business card in my suit. I had gotten her phone number maybe three weeks before and I was scared to talk to her and I remember I woke up that morning. It was about nine in the morning and I just called her right there on the spot. She happened to be at the coffee shop right up the street. We ended up doing an appointment that day and that person blew my business up. She was my first SMD and then promoted another SMD. I hit my $100,000 ring that year, all from starting to talk to people that I was scared to talk to. That also brought me to better people, which meant better markets and better results.

The Future

I want to be the reason why other people's lives are better, whether it's through this business or through philanthropy or through just any means possible; even if it's just a piece of advice in the hallway. I look forward to being 60 years old and looking back on my life and seeing what we were able to do to impact others and my surroundings in a positive way. I want to change my life in a drastic enough way, that it serves my family and humanity in a positive way generationally.

Chapter 9

Paul Hart

My dad was in the military and my mom is Dutch. My dad moved her to the U.S., so they could build a life together. The doctors had told my mom that she was not going to be able to have children, but my parents kept trying and I was born when they were both 42.

It was kind of interesting growing up because my parents were already established emotionally and financially. They'd had 42 years of experience before they raised me. So, I believe I had a great upbringing in terms of stability. My mom ran a little day care at home so she could buy us the stuff that my dad didn't. Not that he couldn't afford it; I just think my dad was so frugal he never wanted us to live like he lived. He grew up in poverty, but he didn't want us in the dangerous areas. I grew up in a middle-income neighborhood but my school was in the lower-middle-income neighborhood. My mom was always at home. So, I think one of the things that kept me safer than most people was that, when I came home, I couldn't get away with anything; there was always somebody there and they always were watching over me. I noticed that a lot of my friends didn't have parents or their parents were both working; so, when my friends came home, they came home to an empty house. As they say, an idle mind is the devil's playground and I see, now, that impact.

I never had a great relationship with my dad because he always worked so hard and when he would get out of work, we'd eat dinner and then he'd rest and watch TV; the traditional family, but I had all the love in the house that I think I ever needed.

My parents wouldn't let me watch rated R movies. I started getting into that stuff at a young age through the other kids. For some reason, it intrigued me. I kind of grew up on the streets because it was my choice. It's not that I didn't have a family; it's just that I was exposed to a life that in some way intrigued me. The fact that my dad was always working played a part. Plus, I had a father and a mother that were the age of most people's grandparents. Everybody's parents were younger than mine and it was weird. That's another reason why I gravitated towards the streets; there is no relation in the teenage mindset when you're a teenager talking to people who are in their 50s and 60s. They could not relate to me and that was very hard. My dad didn't understand the rap music and curse words; he didn't understand why comedians used the F word. I was growing up in the city, being raised by a countryman. So the streets kind of grabbed me and my mentors ended up becoming older people that didn't operate the best way.

With that said I was kind of a leader because I was always going to school and trying to benefit myself. I was always working and trying to make money. I had a paper route when I was 11 or 12 years old. I used to sell golf balls back to the golf course that we lived by and I fixed cars. I loved what it felt like selling golf balls and fixing people's cars, just to have pocket change. It just felt good to make money that I had generated on my own. I still remember that feeling in my heart and it has always sparked the entrepreneurial side of me — even though my dad was an employee and my mom was an ex-social worker. I was always looking for a way to make money without a boss but I was focused on school because my dad told me to go to school; my family and I are very big on education.

When I found this business, it looked like everything that I went through in my life had primed me for it. At the time, I was going to school but I was self-employed as a mechanic. I loved the fact that I could make my own schedule. Nobody had to tell me to work or when to work. I didn't need people to motivate me to make money. All of that combined made me a prime candidate to be an entrepreneur, for the transition to WFG. I didn't need people to motivate me because I was really driven. Despite being big on education, my dad saw how much the opportunity excited me and he completely supported me when I dropped out of college.

As a hard-headed kid growing up, my dad told me "Do things right the first time," "Take pride in your work," and "Be a man of your word." Those comments aggravated me then, but it made me who I am. Today, I shake people's hands, do what I say I'm going to do, and I'm a man of my word.

Introduction To The Company

When I was introduced to the company I had just gotten one of my cars stolen and I was almost completely broke because of all the money I had put into my car. I actually went downtown, with a friend of mine, to go to a bar and have a good time. I ended up bumping into Eric Olson, who my mom used to babysit, when she had her day care business. I recognized him and we talked and kind of made up for old times before we exchanged numbers.

He told me briefly what he did, but I was looking to change my circumstances. So, it didn't really matter what he said. We met on Saturday, but by Tuesday, I got the courage to call him because he hadn't called me. He invited me to the BPM and I ran to Macy's to grab dress clothes so I didn't look like a fool and went to the meeting. Eric introduced me to the speaker, which was Eric Carter. I don't remember much; it wasn't a very high-energy mozone; there wasn't a lot of people making a lot of money. It looked like it then but, now that I look back, the guest count was maybe six or seven… but it sold me the dream because I was predisposed to look for something like it. When I came in, it had all the ingredients of what I was looking for. I've never lost my excitement since that day. I don't know if I've met anybody that's ever been as excited as I was when I went to the BPM and I've been fired up for nine years now.

What Are The Keys To My Personal Success?

The key to personal success is discipline. I think one of the challenges in my life is that I've been a Jack of all trades, expert at none. I tackle something, get good at it, and then I get bored with it; then I tackle something, get good at it and get bored with it. I never really put all my energy into one thing. When I came into this company, it was one of the hardest things I had ever done, leading adults, and I had to really tackle my self- discipline. I think discipline is a matter of making promises and keeping promises when nobody else is watching. It's happened in my diet and exercise, in the way I live my life, my honestly, in my integrity, in my relationship with my wife; it just transcended all different things. So, it's not different in business.

CHAPTER 9
PAUL HART

I didn't know it was going to take me so long to get this off the ground, but I could not sleep until it was done. I'm one of those guys who literally wakes up and rolls out of bed to get my workout in because I told myself that I was going to do it. I have to complete what I start, it's discipline. When you know what you want, discipline is there. If you don't know what you want, it will seem hard to be disciplined.

Common Mistakes Associates Make

Not treating it like a business. I think that's the biggest mistake. Just because it costs $100, I think people treat it like $100 opportunity. For example, a rental car; nobody ever changes the oil on a rental car or washes a rental car because it's not theirs. Once you own something, you treat it a little bit differently.

When I came to this business, I really treated it like it was my business; if there was trash in the bathroom, I would pick up the trash because my guests and teammates might need to use that bathroom. So, I've always treated it as if it were mine. There's a saying: "When the cat's away, the mice will play." Well, when Eric would travel, I looked for that because it was my chance to take ownership in the office.

Chapter 10
Gabie Hart

I grew up in a single-mother home. I'm the youngest of three. My siblings are all seven years apart. I was the baby and also like an only child. Mom was always at work and made sure to provide, no matter what. I love her for that. She taught me hard work was essential to survive. I grew up in a small town near Los Angeles - a city called Bell, far enough from L.A. but, at the same time, still in L.A. - in a predominantly Latino community.

In the third grade, my life changed. My teacher said to me, "You're gifted." I didn't quite know what that meant. She said, "I believe that you belong in the gifted program. Let's test you out." At the time, I didn't know how much that would affect my life, but looking back, I think, *"Wow. That was the first person who believed in me or said that I could do more than I thought."* My mom's time was limited, my sister was in high school busy with sports, my brother moved out and nobody was really around. I got tested, got in, and my associations began to change. I went from the gifted program in my school to getting bussed to magnet schools in Santa Monica, and got a taste of how wealthy people lived. We would drive by these beautiful homes and luxury cars I didn't know how to pronounce. All of my friends, my peers, were either kids of producers, musicians or actors, and I saw a life that I didn't come from, but I definitely wanted.

I believe environment and associations played a major part in who I am now. I didn't want to settle for where we came from. I wanted more than that and, along the way, I fought very hard to be at the top of my class. I had decided I wanted to become a doctor. So, when my choice of high school came, I chose to attend a medical magnet high school in East L.A. My mother married a wonderful man and, unfortunately, at the time, my parents moved away from my school to the suburbs. I attended the local high school. Looking back, everything happens for a reason or I wouldn't be here.

I graduated from high school and then, in my first year of college, I became a single mom. My life completely changed, but definitely for the best. My daughter, Clarissa, made me a stronger woman, a soldier willing to fight harder because of her. I graduated with my Bachelor's degree in Marketing, got my first job in sales and rose to the top; also got into real estate investing.

I met some great people along the way and one of my friends introduced me to another friend, who then introduced me to this business. He didn't introduce me 'til about nine months after he was already in it. I'm not sure if he was afraid of what I would say, because I was pretty excited about where I was in my career. So, timing was not there, but he still brought me to a big event. I didn't care much about it. I just thought: *I'm sure they're having fun, making money; but it's cool, I guess.* Then, about six months later, I went to another big event in San Diego, and that's where I saw many people crossing stage. At that time, my boss at my job had been promoted, somebody else came on and things changed. I no longer liked going to work and I disliked my boss; it was the right time. When I saw people on stage, I said, "If they can do it, I can do it," and that's how I got introduced into the business.

My Personal Challenges

I can't say I've had challenges; at least, my mind doesn't process it that way. I look at a challenge as an obstacle course, and that's exciting for me. I welcome challenges. So, if anything, I knew I had a little girl, my own home, and responsibilities, but I didn't see the challenges. I knew I had to get it done.

My Advice To Young Women In The business?

Simple… Never feel inferior to a man. Always compete. This is the business to do it in. It's all about equality.

What Are The Keys To My Personal Success?

Consistency, discipline, and a burning desire; those are three main things that the winners consistently have. I've noticed that I've moved ahead of everybody else because I'm willing to do our business daily with a clarity about an outcome and my reasons "why".

My Advice To A New Associate

Find someone who believes in you and let them know you

appreciate them for believing. Hopefully, along the way, when it's hard, they'll keep telling you they believe in you.

My Advice To A Leader Who Is Stuck In A Rut

Shed all the bad - kind of like a snake sheds old skin - then a new layer emerges. Let all the bad shed off, start new, and commit to 100% all-in, because anything is possible.

Things I Would Do Differently If I Had To Start Over

I would work on my people skills, soften my edges, and realize that everybody can still win. Even if they are not like me who goes 150 miles an hour, where the normal speed is 70.

Meeting My Spouse In The Business

Our leadership challenged us both to compete for a contest and we both qualified. The first night at the WFG Villa in St. Maarten, our leaders got all of the winners together at an outdoor bar to celebrate. Everybody was having a great time. Then my leader saw what would turn out to be my future husband. We were introduced and it was love at first sight. Four months later, I moved to be closer to him and we made a decision to win together.

The Future

My team's success is of paramount importance. I want to hear their stories of where they were to where they are now and what they have accomplished. I want to see their smile, completely rejoicing in the fact that they stuck through it and all the good that came from it.

Chapter 11

Jaime Villalovos

I was raised in a very, very small town in the north eastern corner of Montana with a population of about 325 people, an hour from the Canadian and North Dakota border, basically, the middle of nowhere. It's a farming community with a very small town mentality. My family was very poor. I am the oldest of six. So, there were a lot of mouths to feed. We grew up using food stamps, welfare and WIC. I remember having to wear hand-me-downs and second-hand clothes from thrift stores. I knew there was no money for college, no opportunity to start the type of life I wanted, and even less opportunity there for women.

There were six of us. I remember my parents never having money to buy anything or pay the bills. I could hear my parents argue about choosing which bill to pay each month and during the freezing Montana winters, what to pay for usually came down to paying for propane to heat our trailer.

Growing up, I knew I didn't want to be poor. I knew at a young age that there was nothing in that town for me. My best options were the barmaid or, if the postal worker died, I may have had a shot at that. Other than that, it was slim pickings for jobs. So, I moved down to California in hopes of getting a good job so I could pay my way through college, help my family and maybe pay my sister's way through college. I remember thinking about other kids trying to go college; how their parents probably saved up money for them to go to school, prepared them for leaving the house, dropping them off at the dorms... the dream scenario. My reality, at the time, was a step-mom who was very ill and a dad who was having a very hard time being in and out of work.

In California, I started working. I got a job at a health club called Bally Total Fitness. I thought it would be an easy, no-brainer type of job where I could make money, go to school, and be in a good environment where people were trying to improve themselves. As I was promoted, I was making more money but was working 10 to 11 hours a day; it became normal to work from 11 a.m. to 11 p.m. So, with the combination of my schedule, plus the very high-pressure corporate type environment, school was out. I stopped going to school and worked full-time with that company for about four and a half years. I kept climbing up that corporate ladder and making more money. By the time I left Bally's, I was making a little under $70,000, but I was very dissatisfied.

I had hit their income ceiling and my distaste for the people I worked with, my horrible schedule, and the feeling of being stuck increased daily. Every day was: get up, go to work, go home, and then go to bed. I felt like I had stopped growing and learning. Deep down, I knew that if I got the chance to do something else, not just anything, but something worth putting my heart into, I would do it. Given the right opportunity, I knew I would work just as hard, make a difference in people's lives, and make more money. But what else was I going to do? I was 22 years old and I didn't finish college. Who was going to give me a shot?

I was so hungry for change, I decided to get into real estate and get licensed. I wanted to finally have control of my time. But, I quickly realized that I didn't want to be driving people around and be at someone's beck and call; not to mention having so many different things outside of my control that directly affected my paycheck. I ended up learning a little bit about mortgages but I still had my full-time job at the gym. All the while, I was growing more and more and more dissatisfied, wanting more out of my life.

One day, a lady came into the gym who I had never met before. I could tell she felt a little out of place so I showed her around. She told me that she had never worked out before and was very intimidated by the gym because she just had her second child. After I showed her around and helped her, she asked, "What do you do? You are so nice and so good with people. Have you ever thought of doing something else?" Her timing couldn't have been better. I was sick and tired of being sick and tired at my job. She invited me to a Saturday morning corporate overview.

As they went through the presentation, they shared who they were and what they did. When the speaker shared with us how they help families, I thought: I need this for myself. I fell in love with the company and all that it stood for. I went full-time within my first few months. I had the conviction that this was where I needed to plant my flag and replace my income and I've been here ever since.

What Are The Keys To My Personal Success?

In the beginning, it was being coachable and finding a mentor. Honestly, I was so young and I knew that I knew nothing; my best chance at being successful was to do exactly what I was coached to do. I was very humble in the fact that I knew nothing about the money business. I knew nothing about the stock market, 401Ks, insurance and securities products, and nothing about real leadership.

I decided to be a sponge and listen to my leader. If he told me to wear purple, I was going to wear purple. Whatever he told me to do, I was going to do it and do it fast. I had a theory. It was called the Pile Theory: His pile of money is bigger than mine and until mine is as big as his, I'm just going to listen to him, and that's what I did. They say: If you want to become a millionaire, find one and do what they do. I was and still am very coachable to my mentors. As soon as I learned our system, I was coachable to that too.

The system was the easiest thing for me to rely on. For a 22-year-old single girl from Montana that moved to California alone, I obviously couldn't go sell to my friends and family. And even if I could, who would see me as a financial advisor? So, I relied 100% on the system to grow my business. Those two things were probably the most important to me in the beginning.

My Advice To A New Associate

Be coachable, find a mentor, and build a good relationship with them... and recruit!! Like I said earlier, I didn't have a market; it was painfully intimidating and tough for me to recruit in the beginning because I was so shy. Talking to a stranger was way outside of my comfort zone; so, to say it was hard for me to recruit in the beginning is an understatement.

I had plenty of excuses not to talk to people but I knew that if I wanted to win, I had to follow the system. I had to grow my business. Looking back at the beginning of my business, my one regret is not going wider. My advice to a new person is to really try to put those natural fears aside, leverage your leaders as much as you can and recruit as much as possible as fast as possible. Even if you think and feel like you don't know what you are doing or don't understand the entire business yet, it's okay. Just keep moving forward, ready or not. Know what you want, why you want it and get after it. More than half the battle is knowing "what" and "why." Even if you don't have a perfect plan, just go for it.

Common Mistakes Associates Make

Some common mistakes would be...hmmm, countless. What I see the most is people not following the system, plain and simple. Being prideful and thinking that maybe they have an easier and faster way is pretty common. Because the system is so simple, most people think they can or need to make it a bit fancier. The same thing - overcomplicating things — happens with the client presentations. I think our system is perfect because of its simplicity. The simpler the system is that you are following, the better, easier, and faster it is to duplicate. Keep it simple in all of your presentations, whether it's a client or recruiting appointment. Over-complication is probably one of the biggest things that holds people back; not being coachable to the system will always slow you down.

Another common mistake is thinking that you've "made it" just because you hit SMD or any other promotion or goal. You constantly have to be growing, evolving, reaching, and thinking bigger. Regularly update your business plan and make it into something that will keep you going when life gets tough. Be aware of who you are associating with on a daily basis. Are the people who you associate with most visionaries or the type of people that keep you thinking and playing small?

My Advice To A Leader Who Is Stuck In A Rut

The first thing I would tell them to do is to sit down, maybe with their spouse, think about, and write down a "possibility list;" also, renew their business plan with new dreams, making sure to have fun they try to figure out something that excites them so they can ignite their own fire.

The next thing I would do if I wanted to get to the next level is reach out to leaders. Reach out to leaders that know you, care about you, and can get you back on the right path and out of your own way. Get in alignment with a vision stretcher.

All of these things are just as important as the next but lastly, I'd get back to basics. Too easily, we get off track with the fundamentals of our business. Read your old notebooks and crack open the BFS book, for starters. I still refer back to my notebooks from when I was a training associate. Seeing the simplicity of the notes that I took and the things that I wrote in the sidelines and the margins to myself became a great tool. Then create a new list and start making phone calls.

When you're in a rut and not doing as much as you know you could, it's easy to look at what others are doing and get down on yourself. We really can be your own worst enemy sometimes. Work on building and believing strong, positive affirmations. When you become stagnant in our business, it is easy to compare yourself to others. Don't beat yourself up. Focus on where you are going, not where you are at. It's critical that you refocus and reenergize YOU during that time.

My Personal Challenges

One of the biggest challenges I had to overcome was myself. When I started in the business, I wasn't a leader. I also wasn't a recruiter or head hunter. I had never done anything like this before. I had a countless number of fears from all of my negative mental programming — but most people get that way as they grow up. I refused to stay that way.

I had such small vision when I started. The biggest I could dream was making the same amount of money I had been making at the gym but having a more flexible schedule. I wasn't thinking I was ever going to be making millions of dollars. Because of that fact, I had to get around the vision stretchers; I had to have people challenge my thinking and go to every big event so that I could start to believe that I could achieve these things.

I had to get over my shyness. I had to get over my fears. I had to self-develop. I had to read books. I had to become a better person in every way I could.

Some of the challenges I face now as a leader are quite different from when I started. When your team starts to grow in other parts of the country like ours has, the challenge is not having those people in your office or state. It can be a challenge having the same influence with them as you do with the ones who live nearby. So, you have to cast a big vision to be able to hold those people. We have to continue to constantly stretch our own vision in order to help others stretch theirs; and sometimes that's tough.

The best part about this business is people. I love watching people come into this business; take Dana Lagattuta, for example; look at the woman that she's become. To see how happy she is because she's fulfilling her dreams, there's nothing better than that. My favorite part of this business is the people. I love our team.

On the other hand, the toughest part about this business can also be people. As a leader, you can sometimes feel you want it more for them than they want it for themselves. You can see further ahead than they can most of the time. Unfortunately, you can't do it for them and sometimes they'll let you down or even hurt your feelings. I learned not to be too emotional about that stuff so I could keep the team moving forward.

My Dream

What Shawn and I are looking forward to the most is living our dream life with our kids. Shawn and I have a clear and common vision of how we want to spend our lives together. We love traveling with our children and creating family memories and family traditions.

For the next few years, we will continue to build our business. We love our team. We will be in the trenches with them and helping families. Eventually, we want to have time freed up to be able to do more charity work. I want to start, or at least help with, a foundation for Autism and other organizations that focus on children with special needs. We've been able to help a foundation get up and running that builds higher self-esteem in young women.

Shawn looks forward to surf trips and living at our beach house where he and the kids will spend longs days out in the waves. The most important thing to us both is to have a strong family. Dream homes, nice cars, and the travel are all great but our true ideal life is being able to enjoy quality time with our family, charity and church service, helping our friends and teammates achieve their dreams, and having complete control of every aspect of our life. I love the lifestyle that this dream business has given our family.

Chapter 12

Shawn Villalovos

I grew up in California in the San Fernando Valley, between Canoga Park and Van Nuys. You could have called us a lower-middle-class family. My dad was in construction as a contractor, and so was my stepdad. We grew up without a lot of money, but my mom did the best she could to provide for us while being a single parent with three kids. My parents split when I was just a couple years old. Mom did a great job with what she had. Along with that, came a lot of moving and bouncing from place to place.

At a young age, I remember feeling like I had to be the man of the house in some ways. Between me and my brother and sister, there is an eight-year gap. So, I always felt like more of a fatherly figure to them than just and older brother. I started working in my grandpa's factory at 12 and worked there until I was about 16, so I could buy a car and not have to work in the factory any more. I was always working. Even before working in the factory, I was that kid in our neighborhood offering to mow people's lawns, clean their pools and do any other odd jobs I could, just to have my own money.

I watched my mom either leave to go to work or come home from work. I used to ask, "Hey Mom, how can I help?" and she would say, "You don't have to help," but then I'd also ask for some money and she'd tell me, "We don't have any money." She told me that, if I wanted money, I had to go work for it. Two of the best things she ever taught me were a solid work ethic and that if I wanted something; I had to work for it.

In high school, I think my mom had big expectations for me because I was a really smart kid; I was in all honors and AP classes, but I hated school. I never told my mom that, but I hated it. Even though school came easily for me, I was one of those kids that teachers got frustrated with because I never applied myself. I just didn't want to be there when I could have been working. So, I stuck to what everyone else in my family did; going to work and getting to work.

When high school was over, I'm pretty sure my mom expected that I was going to try to go to college, but I didn't. Instead, I got into the movie business at 19 years old, working for a company that set up tents for movie locations. I was making more money than all of my friends. So, I thought I had been "discovered." I was doing great, I was making pretty good income and I instantly started spending money on things I didn't need. All of that spending quickly turned into a bunch of debt. What made it worse was that I realized I hated my job and that I couldn't go anywhere else and make the same income without a college degree. I trapped myself in that job and I used to say to myself, "How did this happen to me? I'm 20 years old, in a job I hate and I don't see my position getting any better than this."

My boss promised a lot. For starters, that it was going to get better, I could earn six-figures some day, and that if I just stuck to his coattails things would be great and blah, blah, blah. I started hating that job more and more every day. So, I started asking other people what they did, if there were openings and if they were looking for people.

My mom worked at a custom auto body shop and every Friday night they'd have a bunch of customers and friends come into the shop, mostly just hanging out to get ready for the weekend. One of the regulars was a guy named Steve. My whole family rides motorcycles. So, I remember he always had a really nice motorcycle and I thought: Oh man. What does he do? One day, I finally asked him what he did and if they were looking for people to hire. He said, "Yeah. You know what? Show up to my office, put on a suit and tie and I might be able to get you an interview." He never told me what they actually did. All I knew was that he was a good guy that came into the shop. So, I was invited by a guy I barely knew, to look at a company I'd never heard of before, in an industry I knew absolutely nothing about. I didn't know what I was going to do, quite frankly.

I actually didn't even own a suit and tie. I had to go to Men's Warehouse. I spent about $600 on a suit, tie, shirt, belt and socks combo. Then, the day of, two things happened to me: I realized I didn't know how to tie a tie and I didn't have any nice shoes to wear with the suit. So, literally, I went to my mom's house, had her tie my tie and then I found these old black Nikes that I wore to my graduation at her house and I threw those on and went to our office. I've been with the company ever since. So, it was really kind of chance how I came into it, but I was looking.

I think, at that point, I had been groomed to work hard. Once I saw the company, what we stood for, and what they were about, I loved it! I just happened to go the day that the guy doing the BPM used to be in construction and so he talked about that. All I kept thinking about was how much I related to him and how, if this guy could do it and get out of construction, so could I. I had all these great feelings of, "This could be my shot. This could be my chance." Up until that point in my life, I had always thought I could do something great. I just never felt like I was put in front of the right thing to do that with. So, this was my chance.

What Are The Keys To My Personal Success?

The number one thing is that I married well, in Jamie. In addition to that was constant personal development. I talk about it a lot. I joke about it with my team, but the majority of my team didn't see me in the beginning and how bad I was. Just from a looks standpoint, when I started in the business, I used to have long hair to the middle of my back. I use Spicoli from the movie Fast Times at Ridgemont High as an example. That character was this stereotypical surfer dude and his vocabulary was not strong. He used filler words like the F word, other four letter words and said "dude" every other second; that was me. That's how I spoke. I still sound a little bit like that now but it was 10 times worse back then. Not only that, I was introverted. So, I didn't like talking to people. To this day still, if I go to a gathering or party or something like that, I won't go around the room and meet everybody; I'm not like a social butterfly that way. I'd rather kind of keep to myself, talk to the one or two people that I know well and do that.

So, I really had to learn everything. I mean, most people come in and they think they have to learn financial services and that's going to be the tough part for them, but that was just one of the parts for me. I didn't know anything about finance, didn't know anything about business, didn't know anything about winning, didn't know anything about leadership, didn't know anything about speaking, didn't know anything about sales, or presenting any part of our business. What I do have is an unbelievably positive attitude; that's something I've been blessed with; it's one of my gifts. Then I've always had a long-term perspective on life. So, I never get caught up in kind of short-term difficulties or adversities that have happened in my life. I don't even pay attention that they are happening. I focus on what's on its way. So, those are the only real gifts I had starting in the business. I had to get good at everything necessary to win here.

I think the key to that was learning what those things were and what to do and how to win at the highest levels. After that, just work every single day at getting better at those things and practicing and being uncomfortable. Speaking is probably the one that stands out the most because speaking was what I needed to practice and what makes me the most uncomfortable. Speaking one-on-one and in people's houses sitting with them; that, sometimes, was more difficult than speaking in front of a group for me.

So, I'd go into appointments and sweat like crazy, I would shake, I would stutter, I would lose the feeling in my hands and my feet; my ears and my nose would literally go numb and by the time I'd leave the appointment. It could be 90 degrees out, I'd be freezing cold because, for whatever reason, my body would just go into this weird thing that it would do. But I persevered, pushed through that stuff, improved and then literally, out of nowhere about five or six years later, I just stopped doing it. So, instead of focusing on the things I couldn't control, I focused on the thing that I could, which was constantly getting better.

My Advice To A New Associate

Listen to the people training you, especially your SMD. Unless they are totally out of alignment with your leadership, your CEOs and your EVCs. Listen to what they're telling you because they have a vested interest in your success. They are never going to do anything that's not going to help you grow and achieve success. They are going to show you the fastest possible way to do it and the only way you are going to slow yourself down is by trying to do it your own way, not listening to them, or coming up with some unique idea that you think will be better.

Understand the person training you is not just taking their personal experience and giving you that. They are taking the combined experience of hundreds of years of all of the best people in our industry, what's worked, and what hasn't worked and giving you, specifically, the things that have worked the best and the fastest. So, all you really have to do is go out and do those things. Listening better and implementing faster is what will give you your best and fastest chance of success here.

My Advice To A Leader Who Is Stuck In A Rut

Build you business from big event to big event. As far as leadership goes, not being good at any of the stuff starting out, I had to learn how to do that. I was very coachable and because I listened to the person that was teaching me what to do, other people looked at it as if my leaders were taking advantage of me. We were going out on appointments and doing field training and sales were happening and they were making a lot of money in that process through my market, the people that I knew... but they were also building me a team and an organization.

Within a year, I still wasn't making much money but had 30 to 40 people showing up to be BPMs on my team, every single week.

I now had this team that was looking for leadership. My SMD did a lot of that but I also started to realize I had to start doing a lot of that because he had other legs and other teams that he was working with. I also realized that I had to become more of a leader if I wanted to grow faster and if I expected those people to go out on field trainings and do that stuff with me once I was licensed. I think that my biggest advantage was having big events to go to where it wasn't just my SMD that I was listening to. The big events were where I got to hear a good cross-pollination of a lot of different teams and hierarchies and leaders across the company and leaders in general. Going to conventions and hearing a Norman Schwarzkopf speaker, a Lou Holtz speaker or somebody like that and learning their tips on things that help improve leadership abilities as well as reading good books is key. John Maxwell's books are probably the number one things that come to mind when thinking of leadership.

So, again, back to the self-improvement and working on yourself. It's not enough to read the books on leadership and to try to get better at leadership. You have to surround yourself with people that are leaders in this specific company, in your specific field and see what's working for them. Live through their personal examples and be around them and build relationships with them. And so, I know this is a long answer but to wrap it all up: The fastest way through those big events is by osmosis and being around them.

Sitting here, I am thinking about one of the biggest changes for me in increasing my personal leadership development and that was going on the Hawaii trip with the company. I was still broke and went on the trip and I didn't have any money. I was a senior associate at the time. I met Jeff when we first got off the bus for that trip. He was the first person we saw and met. Jeff said, "Hey," and started talking to Jaime and I and it was just being around him on that trip. We were also introduced to other leaders, but I think he was the biggest one who sat down and talked with us, helped us, trained us, answered questions, and really helped us develop into better leaders by association.

Things I Would Do Differently If I Had To Start Over

I'd go wider faster. Realistically, I wouldn't change the people that have come in or out of our organization, the mistakes we've made or any of that stuff. I mean, all of that served a purpose and not just giving us the business we have today. It all made us the people that we are today and gave us the friendships we have. The one thing I would change is: I would've gone and talked to more people than I did to bring them into my business directly. That's the only difference. If we had talked to twice as many people back then, our business would be twice as big now; if we had talked to three times as many it, would be three times larger; 10 times more people and our business would be 10 times as large as it is now. Everything else happened the way it was supposed to. So, just adding more people earlier on would have been a much greater advantage. Again, no regrets through it, but that would have definitely made a larger impact overall in overall growth.

The Future

Well, Jaime and I, we have it in writing — our ideal life — and that includes the ideal schedule. It's the ideal and we've put a lot of thought into it. It's been months and months and it's still evolving and improving but it's something we think a lot about. When I was newer in the business, I had my top 10 goals. One of them was to have this house on the beach and I knew which beach, I knew how large I wanted the house, how many kids I wanted to have, and part of it was always having a great wife. Jaime and I are in the process of getting that home. In the next couple of years, we will have that home on the beach and will write a check for it.

For us, it's really not about the big, nice, elaborate things, houses, cars, etc. We've had that stuff and gotten rid of some of that stuff, but more than anything, it's about our lifestyle and the balance we have, our relationship strength and how that constantly improves; how our spiritual faith is always getting stronger, and then just the time allotment of how we spend our time with each other and with our family. For me, it's really a dream come true; being able to do the things that I got into the business for. One of the biggest ones was I was willing to be temporarily motivated to be permanently lazy. I think naturally I'm a lazy guy but I was willing to do whatever to get into a position where I could be that way. The funny thing is that now we're in that position, but we're not lazy. We've still got to be doing something, but we definitely do the things we like to do.

I've changed a lot in this business. I couldn't even imagine still being the same. It scares me. I get chills thinking about what I'd be like if I hadn't been introduced to this business. At the same time, I haven't changed a lot. I still enjoy surfing. I still like throwing on some flip-flops, shorts, and a T-shirt and walking around town. It's not like I still don't do that. I think, for me, the dream lifestyle is that I can still be myself and still have a business in financial services and be treated and looked at as a professional. At the same time, I can also walk around in flip-flops and go for surf every now and then and be with my family and be natural with them. I think one of the greatest compliments about our lifestyle we've received from people who have had a chance to be around us is people always say, "Man, it's so cool being around you guys because you are actually normal people." I don't really necessarily know what that means, but I think what it means is that we are ourselves. We do things that we enjoy. We don't do things that we think other people are going to think are cool or like. We don't want to live in a place because we think other people would think it's a cool or a nice house or any of that stuff. I want to live in a place because it's one of the best point breaks for surfing in the entire world and I happen to want to not only be able to surf, but also to be able to enjoy those things with my family. It's a controlled environment, it's a gated community on the beach, and there are only a few houses there and, of those few, almost nobody lives there full-time. So, you have your own environment for your kids to run around and we'll have the house that all of their friends are going to want to be at. You get to control your environment; meaning knowing where your kids are, knowing that your place is the place that they want to be in, having a haven to raise your family. It's more than just the house or the location or any of that stuff; it's a combination of having a strong spiritual and family life with those things.

So, if I were to sell you the dream on that, that's different for everybody. For us, it was that, more than anything, creating an environment where our family could be strong and grow stronger together and on our own terms. Just not having to punch a clock, not having to be at meetings is all we ever wanted. To this day it's funny, friends that I went to school with or that I used to hang with and they say, "Hey, what are you doing this weekend?" and I say, "I'm going to a retreat in Arizona," to which they say, "Oh, really. Is that like a company thing?" and then I say, "Yeah. It's a company thing," and they are like, "Man, that's too bad." They just don't get it; they don't understand how great it is. You get to be around champions, people that are winning in their lives, or who want to be, and the thought process is so different; nobody comes to events of ours, dragging themselves in thinking, "Oh man, I've got to go to work. I've got to go to this deal." That's a great life when you can get up excited and vibrant about not only making your dreams come true but helping other people do the same. The excitement and buzz that's in the room in that process, that never gets old. You're truly making a difference in people's lives; you can go to sleep at night feeling great about it; you can wake up every day feeling great about it; and, in that process, you become the person you always wanted to be and are able to do the things you always wanted to do.

Chapter 13

Eric Olson

I was born and raised in San Jose, California. As a little kid, I had a great family - great parents and great siblings. I'm the oldest of four children. I have two little brothers who are a lot younger than me, and I was their role model and mentor.

I've been playing sports my entire life, ever since I was five years old. I played baseball, basketball, and football. For 18 straight years that's all I did, played sports year-round. I was on travel teams, all-star teams, and I always wanted to be the best. I always tried to get better every single year because I always thought I wanted to be a professional athlete. I didn't know if it was going to be football or basketball or baseball, but I definitely wanted to be a professional athlete.

Out of high school, I got a full scholarship to play football at San Jose State University. I was one of the only kids from my high school to ever get a full Division I scholarship for football. I played football for about four years and had a great time. Then I was introduced to this business by a friend of mine. She decided it wasn't for her, but she put me down as a quality referral. I joined the company back in May of 2003 while I was still playing football, going to college and working a little job at the airport. I was coaching and doing 10 things at once.

Then, I went to a big event. You know what they say: "You can't change people, but you can bring them to life-changing events." This event, RBCL University 2004 in Georgia, sold me the dream and forced me to make a life-changing decision. I quit everything in my life; I dropped out of college, quit the football team, quit my job, stopped coaching and decided to go full-time, 100% in this business. So, I went from, "I hope this business works" to "I have to make it work, no matter what. I better make it here or they are going to be sending flowers because I am going to die trying."

Because my little brothers were like my kids, I was always mentoring, coaching and helping them. I thought that when I had kids of my own one day, I wanted to be there for my kids and coach and mentor them in the same way. I now have two little boys of my own, Jeremiah Champion Olson and Cameron Elijah Olson, who I love very much. This really attracted me to the business because you have freedom of time. You can spend time with your kids and have a great life. That's one of the things that attracted me to the business and again when I decided to go full-time I went from, "I hope this works" to "I have to make it work, no matter what, 100%." I went full-time in 2004, got licensed and the rest is history.

What Are The Keys To My Personal Success?

After doing this business for about 10 years, I think there are many things that have helped me to become successful. One of those things is mental toughness. That's a big part of this business. You've got to be mentally tough, not physically tough; make sure you are mentally tough. It is very important and I think that is one of my biggest strengths.

Another key is being very competitive, wanting to win and having a burning desire to be successful; making sure that I was going to be successful.

I also think that being part of a team in sports helped me to be coachable to a leader. We have great leaders in the company. So, being coachable helped me learn at the speed of instruction.

Finally, having a great work ethic helped a great deal too. I learned that from my parents who both had jobs and owned their own businesses as well. I tell people that I only work half days... 12 hours a day.

My Personal Challenges

Well, one of the things is that I was 3,000 miles away from most of my leaders. I had to do this business on my own without a mentor, without a leader close by starting out. That was difficult and I made a lot of mistakes that I wouldn't have made had I had a leader closer. In the end, it made me much stronger as a leader. Find a mentor or leader as quickly as you can so you can avoid some of those early pitfalls. They have already made those mistakes and will save you the time and the headache of making them yourself.

Another thing is that I never really had to study too much for tests in high school and college. I would always pass without a problem. The tests here really need study time. I failed six different times on the Life & Health, Series 6 and Series 63 exams. I didn't get securities licensed until I was in the business almost three years. Failing my securities exams multiple times and not having a leader / mentor close to me to help me through that challenge was a big struggle for me.

My Advice To A New Associate

Find a mentor, a leader that is willing to help, coach and teach you. Make sure you respect that person; make sure that you meet them halfway so that they will take you the other half of the way.

You must know the system, accept the system and run the system. You also have to trust that the system works. It has created many millionaires, including me. I became a millionaire in this great company before I was 30 years old. Trust the system and know that it works.

I'd recommend just believing that you can do it. It probably took me 14 months in the company to even start believing that I could do it. That's when the business really took off for me and I was never the same after that. So, just believe that you can do it right away, have a leader / mentor who is willing to coach you and make sure you get after it as fast as you possibly can, trust the system and run the system.

Common Mistakes Associates Make

The most common mistake people make: they are thinking too much. Instead of doing, they are thinking. Knowledge is not power, unless it's applied. There is something called "IQ" in the business. I call it "Implementation Quotient." It's how fast you implement the things you learn that really matter. It's not just learning things; it's implementing what you learn right away. So, I think a lot of new people are not implementing what they learn right away. If you learn how to recruit, you've got to start recruiting. If you learn how to prospect, make calls or run appointments, you've got to implement that right away while it's fresh in your mind.

I think people need to stop thinking so much and just start doing more. Some people think it's the more you learn, the more you do; but, really, it's the more you do the more you learn. Stop thinking and just start doing.

My Advice To A Leader Who Is Stuck In A Rut

I'd tell them to look in the mirror and be happy with how far they've come from where they started; to know that this business is unlimited opportunity, unlimited growth and unlimited income; that they really shouldn't try to be other people or some of the best leaders in the company but rather the best version of themselves. I would recommend they look in the mirror again and not only focus on their strengths but also their weaknesses; just be very candid and acknowledge what needs to be fixed to get better. Be more energetic, be more excited, be more fired up and just be better. I think just being the very best version or an upgraded version of oneself will make all the difference in the world as a leader. For example, I realized that I had to get healthy. So, I lost 150 pounds in the last nine months.

Things I Would Do Differently If I Had To Start Over

Number one: They say, "Build leaders and teams will come," but you've got to build yourself before you build others. So, focus on building yourself right away and get better with personal development and self-improvement by listening to audio CDs, reading the right books, and hanging out with the right people from day one. That will really help a lot.

Number two: After you've built yourself as a leader, start building others. Build your leaders and the teams will come. The more leaders you have on your team, the faster you will get to the top. The most important thing in this business, in my opinion, is building leaders. If you help other people get to where they want to go, you'll get to where you want to go. So, right away, aggressively start trying to build seven to ten key leaders direct to you. When you start building them, helping them out, and getting them to where they want to go, they will get you where you want to go. Don't just throw people up against the wall and hope they stick. Instead, really lock on to people faster and better, and get them to the top of the company as fast as you can so then you can get there, also.

My Dream

Well, one of my goals was to be a millionaire before I was 30 years old; and I hit that goal, and that was very exciting for me. I feel like I had to set the pace for my team because, if I stop at $1.8 million a year, where I am now, then my team is going to stop at half of what I do. So, I feel like I have to sell a big dream, sell a big vision, and always be on my "A" game so that my team follows me and respects me at the same time.

My goal, my ultimate goal, is to make $1 million a month before I turn 40. One of my main reasons is that I know my team will be right there with me at $7, $8, $9, $10 million a year. We have unlimited opportunity, unlimited income potential here in our business, and we might as well take advantage of that.

Art Williams was TBE - The Best Ever - in this business, and that's really my goal: to be the best ever. Art Williams had 250,000 licensed agents on his team. It's my goal to have 251,000 licensed agents on my team and just be the best that there ever was; that's ultimately my goal.

So, to make a million dollars a month before I turn 40, I want to create 1,000 millionaires on my team, which will make me a billionaire by the age of 60. That's the goal: Create 1,000 millionaires on my team and then I become a billionaire.

That's just exciting to think about: To be able to be the go-to person in my family and to be well respected by all of me peers, all while doing incredible things and breaking records. I can be at the top of the company and make a great difference as a leader to a lot of people.

I have a couple of other goals, too. Number one: I want to make sure that I impact people's lives in a positive way, and that they feel like they are better people because I am their leader; that they are better all around. Number two: I want to help my leaders create profitable, sustainable, long-term businesses. I genuinely want to help people to do that.

I was thrilled to be the Legacy Team MVP in 2013...
I'm excited to be getting my $2,000,000 ring...

I will earn my SEVC promotion at this year's convention in 2014!

CHAPTER13
ERIC OLSON

Chapter 14
Greg Kapp

Before I begin, Tina and I want to publicly thank Jeff Levitan for all the time, money and sacrifice it took to get this book published. I believe this book was divinely inspired because these success stories will inspire tens of thousands of people long after we are gone.

We also want to thank our dear friend Cam Levitan who sacrifices so much every day, taking such loving care of the Levitan family. Imagine being the mother to four babies, all less than six years old, while your Superman husband is out trying to save the world. We love you Jeff and Cam.

My Story

I grew up in Milwaukee, Wisconsin, over 60 years ago, in a middle-class family where I was taught hard work and integrity. I grew up shy, spending most of my childhood trying not to make mistakes because I had a well developed fear of failure. I successfully went through four years of high school, hiding behind other students so I wouldn't get called on to speak. I didn't go on a date until I was 20.

Continuing with that mindset, I took a job at the post office at age 22 because the work was easy and I was never expected to step out of my comfort zone. I worked at the post office for 15 uneventful years. Tina and I had two daughters and I began to count down the years until retirement. I pretty much accepted that my life would be one of mediocrity.

One day, my boss, Al Schwartz, showed me a small *Time* magazine article about a former football coach named Art Williams who had started a financial services company in Atlanta where you could start part-time. I decided to write a short note, asking for information on how I could get involved. About a month later, I got a call from the number one earner in the company and he sent me two airline tickets to come down to Atlanta to check things out. When we got there, he drove us over to meet with Art Williams. My wife and I were completely overwhelmed, even before I filled out my A.M.A.

My leader told me that he was going to fly his jet up to Milwaukee on the following Tuesday and that I should invite family and friends over to our home for a 90-minute company overview. We had 13 people there. He presented and all 13 joined and bought products that night. I thought to myself: *This business is so easy. I will be an overnight success.* NOT EXACTLY!

The next five years were the most difficult, challenging and frustrating that I ever could have imagined. My leader flew back to Atlanta and I had no one to present the overview for me, no one to help train my associates, no one to help me make phone calls or to field train me. We couldn't even afford an office. So, I worked out of my home for the first five years.

I was a wreck. I wanted to quit so many times. I was so far out of my comfort zone; my heart would beat so fast I thought I was having a heart attack. I was living a daily nightmare. We had built and lost five different teams. In my 5th year, my cash flow was only $22,000.

Something was happening to me from the inside out as I continued to read good books. Because I had to do everything myself, I was being forced to change, forced to grow, forced to develop new success habits and a strong faith. By our 7th year, we qualified for the $100,000 ring. Then our income and our team exploded. Today, we have six EVCs and eight CEOs. Tina and I now live a dream lifestyle with our children and grandchildren in Florida. We are at the "Massive Passive" income stage.

What Are The Keys To My Personal Success?

My number one secret is my strong faith in God. My second secret has been the unconditional love and support of my wife, Tina, who, as of this writing, has been married to me for 39 wonderful years. Tina believed in me when I didn't even believe in myself. Someone on our team who reminds me a lot of Tina is Stacy Stokes, Michael Stokes' awesome wife.

When I started the business, I was well developed in worry, doubt and fear. These three emotions were all self-destructive. When I learned that fear of rejection and fears of failure were processes of accepting a lie as if it were the truth, I knew I had to change my mindset. My strong faith has replaced the worry, the self-doubt, and the small, useless thoughts I used to permit into my mind.

At some point on my journey, I realized that inner peace was my birthright. Following my Bible and the instructions laid out in the book Think and Grow Rich, I have learned to control my subconscious mind. If you truly desire complete freedom, learn to take control of the only two things our creator gave us complete control over: our mind (thoughts) and our emotions (feelings).

As I learned to control my thoughts and feelings, I replaced several poor habits with success habits. Confucius once said, "Human beings are very similar. What separates them are their habits." Rather than procrastinate, I learned to say, "Do it now," or "What's important now?" I ended my habit of making excuses and blaming others by taking full responsibility for my life. Two great leaders who I have observed replace old poor habits with new world-class habits are Paul Hart and Juan Jaime.

The final key to my success is how I have learned to handle all adversity. The Bible instructs us to treat all of our trials like they are as precious as gold. Low self-esteem people permit adversity to steal their momentum, while high self-esteem leaders leverage every adversity as a reminder to double-down their focus on their goals. At some point, a person must realize that adversity is not random. Adversity is ruthless. While it does make the weak, weaker, the converse is true: adversity makes the strong, stronger.

My Advice To A New Associate

First of all, learn to get comfortable being uncomfortable. This business will constantly stretch you and force you to grow. Unfortunately, most people are programmed to fail. So, as soon as they get challenged to get out of their comfort zone, many quit. This is why our entire industry has such a high turnover rate. It takes a high self-esteem individual to handle the rejection. When I think of some wonderful couples that I have seen continue to grow over long periods of time, I think of Shawn and Jaime Villalovos and Jeff and Marcy Blochowiak.

Secondly, I would highly recommend you do what all successful people do: suspend you disbelief until you are able to develop your own belief. Learn to borrow your leader's belief. I watched two of my good friends, Elan Michael and David Horenstein, suspend their disbelief when they first joined our company.

The third advice I would give you is to do exactly what Jeff Levitan did from day one. On day one, Jeff turned his warm list over to me to work for him. He realized early that he had trust with his warm market, but he had no credibility. Jeff got out of his own way. He let me build the business for him while he farmed friendships and added new names to his prospect list.

Jeff Levitan always moved at the speed of my instructions. He would observe every appointment like it was his last. He observed with the intention of doing it himself quickly. He watched intently as I presented, fast-started, tap-rooted, and sold. Jeff took ownership immediately; he knew his training period was temporary. I have never had to tell Jeff something twice. That's why my mentor, Rich Thawley, took Jeff under his wing early; Jeff displayed leadership. Take ownership right away. This is your business. Force your leaders to take an interest in mentoring you.

I strongly suggest that you learn the "Nobility Exchange" by getting the person who brought you into the business to their next promotion. Jeff Levitan was legendary when he publicly stated, "I will not rest until my leader Greg Kapp is a CEO!" Tina and I will be forever grateful to Jeff for all he has unselfishly done for us. Another good example of someone who has always been aligned is Marla Isisdro. Since day one, she has always been fiercely loyal to John Shin, Jeff and myself.

Lastly, I would recommend that you develop the great habit of being a person of your word. My father taught me that my word was all that I'd ever really have. The greatest example of this habit is the 2013 WFG-MVP Eric Olson. Eric Olson is a man of few words but when he tells me anything, I know he will hit his goals, every time.

My Advice To a Leader Who Is Stuck In A Rut

My initial advice to leaders who find themselves in a rut is to find a way to get re-inspired. Remember: If you have lost your vision for the future, you have no power in the present.

Life and business are continuous cycles of beginnings, endings, and then new beginnings. We must all learn to let go of past baggage that is clouding up our future vision. We all make mistakes, get offended, get ripped off, and experience betrayal by our friends. Always remember that bitterness is worse than betrayal. Don't permit your history to define your destiny.

One of my favorite scriptures is 2 Corinthians 5:17. "Old things have passed away and all things have become new." I remember when John Shin was frustrated by the way his former leadership was treating him. We are so blessed to have his team in our hierarchy now. John didn't get bitter; he got better and was voted the MVP of WFG four years in a row. He was able to get past his past and stay in the now. My question is: Can you move on from your past?

I watched Randy Sicairos do the same thing. He had some unfair things happen to him and thought about quitting. I called Randy and told him that something similar had happened to me and I gave him some biblical wisdom. I shared with Randy that

Proverbs 6:30-31 says that if anything is ever taken from you, you should first forgive the ones who did it and then claim a sevenfold return on whatever was taken. I proudly watched as Randy took my advice. He is now a CEO team and one of the fastest growing teams in the company.

Common Mistakes Associates Make

A common mistake I see a lot of people make is once they have teammates, they slow down their personal activity and try to manage their team. When you manage or micromanage your own team, you will find that the low self-esteem associates love it but the high self-esteem teammates want to be led, not managed. You end up retaining low self-esteem, high maintenance people while you end up driving away the people you really want — the results-oriented leaders. One of the best compliments Jeff Levitan gave me was when he said, "Greg, I have always appreciated that you never tried to control or micromanage me. You led by your example and were always there for me, but gave me freedom to run my business myself, giving me freedom to make my own mistakes and to grow my own business."

I am so grateful my leader had the wisdom to stay out of my way and gave me the freedom to make my own mistakes. A secret to duplication is that the great principles of our business are never taught, they are caught.

A second big mistake I see people make, and this advice includes the leaders stuck in a rut, is that they stop growing. In the Bible, Romans 12:2 says, "Be not conformed to this world, but be transformed by the renewing of your mind." The word conformed in this context could be similar to a Jello-mold. Many people in our company have their minds conformed to a failure mindset. Their thoughts have been molded by their fears, worries, doubts and small thinking. In order to break that mold, the Bible instructs us to continuously renew our minds. We must be careful to whom we are listening because the messenger may leave but the negative message lingers. We must focus on solutions, not problems; focus on goals and not circumstances. We also have to stop the habit of worrying about what other people think.

A third mistake I see many people make, whose dream started out to be financially independent, is that when the system doesn't seem to work for them, they spend most of their time mastering becoming a financial planner. That may be a great strategy, until you find you have few or no warm leads. I was taught from day one that working in a cold market will create lots of activity with very little results. What is your time worth? You see, my goal was always to master the distribution of financial products because I would much rather earn 1% of 100 people's effort, than 100% of my own effort. This is something at which I have seen Rob Day excel.

My Dream

I have not shared my deep-rooted dream publicly before. Even though I was very honored to meet Art Williams my first day in the business, I did not see this business as my destiny. I was not intrigued by all the income and rewards they originally spoke to me about because I had already decided that I would one day become a pastor. As I continued to pray about my future, the Lord spoke in to my heart that this business was my calling, not being a pastor. He led me to a scripture in Proverbs 13:22. It says, "The wealth of the wicked is being laid up for the righteous." This is the Bible's prophecy about a huge wealth transfer. God also revealed to me that my worry, doubt, and small thinking were sabotaging my own destiny. That's why I developed strong faith to overcome my poorly conformed mindset. That's why my wife and I know that Jeff Levitan was a gift from God to us. He is strong in all the areas in which I am weak.

This entire movement, which began with Art Williams in 1977, continued with Aegon purchasing Transamerica in 1999, and then purchasing our entire distribution team in 2001. These are not a coincidence. Now, with Aegon's unlimited backing, the tremendous retail platform of Transamerica — an independent product mix that is second to none — and the greatest system of finding and developing leaders ever known to mankind, we are ready to explode in 2014.

I consider 1977-2013 to be our practice era. I believe, with all my heart, that our company hasn't even attracted its best leaders yet. My vision is that, soon, you will see well-known former athletes, coaches, and celebrities join our movement. There are millions of high self-esteem unemployed and underemployed people who will realize that not finding a good job was a blessing in disguise because it helped them to find us. I predict that companies with hundreds and thousands of individuals in real estate, accounting, tax preparation, mortgages and so on will be merging their business model with ours, at no expense to them. I have a vision where leaders who have made millions in other companies and industries will be led by God to bring their connections and expertise to our wealth transference movement.

In closing, I thank God for His vision, direction and favor. I thank Tina for nearly 40 years of marital bliss, with a high expectation of 40 more years. I thank our three children — Elizabeth, Rebecca and Jessie — for all the sacrifices they have had to make in this 27-year journey and I want to thank our grandchildren — Joshua and Sophia — who inspire Granny and Papa every day.

Tina and I thank Jeff and Cam for their unwavering love and loyalty. Last, but not least, we thank all the leaders and associates of our Legacy team. I may be biased but I know, deep in my heart, we have the greatest team ever assembled.

Conclusion

It is always amazing to watch ordinary people accomplish extraordinary things. We are reminded and perhaps encouraged to reach further and dream bigger. Success is not as elusive as most people think it is. There is a recipe for success and you just need the right ingredients. Ingredients like a burning desire and a strong commitment are a good starting point. It is necessary to start with the end in mind to be constantly reminded of why we are working so hard and pushing through challenges. The right tools for the job are always crucial to an excellent finished product. Our great company has spent decades and millions of dollars developing all the necessary tools for the job. Then we need a proven system and a good coach who has been there and done that. Everyone needs a coach in the game who is willing to roll up their sleeves and get their hands dirty too. That's the major difference between management and true leadership. The success recipe would also have cooking times, you can't rush excellence. It requires time to build a great business and sometimes you even have to start over from scratch. At the end, wouldn't it be worth it to have a successful business that could possibly create generational wealth, and provide for you and you loved ones; even if it took years to accomplish? Of course it would be worth it! The good news is that during the time it takes to build your business, you will be improving yourself through personal development and helping other people. What a worthwhile cause! You can also include, not exclude, your family and friends if you choose to do so. Most businesses are exclusive not inclusive. Therefore the need or desire to get away from work to spend time socializing with those you care about no longer exists. You can do it all in one place. What a way to enjoy that precious journey called LIFE. Most people desire either a life of happiness or a life of purpose. Here you can have both! Our compensation is directly proportionate to the number of people we help accomplish their goals. In my humble opinion, this is the best place to make the most out of your life and get the most out of your time!

Disclaimer & Copyright Page

The commentaries and views expressed in this book are for information and/or motivational purposes only. The views and opinions expressed therein are those of the individuals and author.

Disclaimer

Published by: Empower Media, Inc.

Made in the USA
Columbia, SC
20 May 2018